CW00801596

THE IBA GUIDELINES ON PARTY REPRESENTATION IN INTERNATIONAL ARBITRATION

The Guidelines on Party Representation are one of three key publications published by the IBA and are commonly referred to or adopted as good practice in international arbitration. This user-friendly handbook to the guidelines will benefit the understanding and practical application of arbitration protocol in the legal community. Written by a respected and experienced arbitration practitioner, this is a companion volume to The IBA Rules on the Taking of Evidence in International Arbitration and combines commentary from the drafting committee, additional analysis of the guidelines and tabular comparative material addressing the interaction with Major Professional Conduct Rules and Major Institutional Rules. It is a convenient and invaluable resource for best practice on the duties of arbitrators, institutions and other representatives in this field.

PETER ASHFORD is head of the International Arbitration Group at Fox Williams LLP.

THE IBA GUIDELINES ON PARTY REPRESENTATION IN INTERNATIONAL ARBITRATION

A Guide

PETER ASHFORD

Fox Williams LLP

CAMBRIDGE
UNIVERSITY PRESS

University Printing House, Cambridge CB2 8BS, United Kingdom

Cambridge University Press is part of the University of Cambridge.

It furthers the University's mission by disseminating knowledge in the pursuit of education, learning, and research at the highest international levels of excellence.

www.cambridge.org
Information on this title: www.cambridge.org/9781107161665

© Peter Ashford 2016

This publication is in copyright. Subject to statutory exception and to the provisions of relevant collective licensing agreements, no reproduction of any part may take place without the written permission of Cambridge University Press.

First published 2016

Printed in the United Kingdom by Clays, St Ives plc

A catalogue record for this publication is available from the British Library.

Library of Congress Cataloging-in-Publication Data
Ashford, Peter, author.
The IBA guidelines on party representation in international arbitration :
a guide / Peter Ashford, Fox Williams LLP.
International Bar Association guidelines on party representation
in international arbitration
Cambridge, United Kingdom : Cambridge University Press, 2016. | Includes
bibliographical references and index.
LCCN 2016021870 | ISBN 9781107161665 (hardback)
LCSH: International Bar Association. IBA guidelines on party representation
in international arbitration. | International commercial arbitration. | Practice
of law. | BISAC: LAW / Arbitration, Negotiation, Mediation.
LCC K2400 .A9835 2016 | DDC 347/.09–dc23
LC record available at https://lccn.loc.gov/2016021870

ISBN 978-1-107-16166-5 Hardback

Cambridge University Press has no responsibility for the persistence or accuracy of URLs for external or third-party Internet Web sites referred to in this publication and does not guarantee that any content on such Web sites is, or will remain, accurate or appropriate.

Contents

Contents

IBA Guidelines on
Party Representation in
International Arbitration
Adopted by a resolution of
the IBA Council
25 May 2013
International Bar Association

Preface and dedication

This book goes to the publishers as the 2015 International Arbitration Survey by White & Case/Queen Mary University of London is published. It finds international arbitration as popular as ever and the international arbitration community in rude health. Respondents to the survey felt that there was adequate regulation but nevertheless called for more 'micro-regulation' of third-party funding, tribunal secretaries and conduct of arbitrators. The survey also found something of a 'due process paranoia' causing increased cost and delay.

It is certainly not for this book to suggest that parties and tribunals routinely formally adopt the Guidelines. Rather, the adequacy of existing regulation is endorsed, as is the notion that parties and tribunals should craft a process around the true issues that require to be determined: a process that meets the parties' objectives of time and cost (to the extent that any consensus is possible after the dispute has arisen) and, in doing so, becomes a pragmatic and cost-efficient process, being guided as necessary by the Guidelines and other soft law.

One of the inherent benefits of arbitration – the ability to craft a bespoke process to meet the needs of the situation – has the potential to be lost in the tidal wave of soft law and, as the survey terms it, 'due process paranoia'. It may be a forlorn hope that those inherent benefits will again come to the fore – but we can dream.

The structure of the book is to set out the Guidelines (in bold) and Committee Comments (in italics) with a discussion following each section. The divisions within the original Guidelines and Committee Comments do not permit individual Guidelines (as opposed to the original grouping) to be commented upon; and, in any event, the original grouping provides a logical split. Within the discussion, subheadings are inserted to assist the reader.

I gratefully acknowledge the help, support and guidance from my partners at Fox Williams and from friends and colleagues who have debated issues with me (whether knowingly for this book or not). Special thanks go to my colleagues, Sabrina Janzik, and Jeremy McKeown at Fox Williams, whose valuable work on the tables in the Appendices and the case index respectively, and for other parts of the text, has been most helpful. As usual, however, all errors and omissions are mine alone.

Finally, the task of producing a book such as this is impossible without the love and encouragement of those closest to you. As my rock and constant support, this book is dedicated to my wife, Susan, and our children Amy, Hannah and Kate.

Cases

Ali Shipping Corp v. *Shipyard Trogir* [2007] EWCA Civ 3054

Arrow Nominees Inc. v. *Blackledge* [2001] BCC 591

Attia v. *Audionamix Inc.* 14 Civ 706 (S.D.N.Y. 21 September 2015)

Bak v. *MCL Financial Group Inc.* 88 Cal. Rptr. 3d 800 (Cal. App. 2009)

Bennett v. *Bayes* (1860) 5 H&N 391

Berkley Community Villages v. *Pullen* [2007] EWHC 1130 (Ch)

British American Tobacco Australia Services v. *Cowell* [2002] CA (Vic) 2002-12-06

Bullis v. *Nichols* [2005] WL 1838634 (W.D. Wash. 1 August 2005)

Carter v. *Boehm* (1766) 3 Burr 1905, 1910

CBC Oppenheimer Corp. v. *Friedman* WL 244820 (Cal. App. 2002)

Central Estates (Belgravia) Ltd v. *Woolgar* [1972] 1 Q.B. 48

Compagnie Europeene de Cereals SA v. *Tradax Export* [1986] 2 Lloyd's Rep. 301

Decision Regarding the Practices Used to Prepare and Familiarise Witnesses for Giving Testimony at Trial No. ICC-01/04-01/06, 30 November 2007

Department of Economic Policy and Development of the City of Moscow v. *Bankers Trust Co.* [2004] EWCA Civ 314

Digicel v. *Cable & Wireless* [2008] EWHC 2522 (Ch)

Douglas v. *Hello* [2003] EWHC 55 (Ch)

Emmott v. *Michael Wilson & Partners* [2008] EWCA Civ 184

Esso Petroleum Co. Ltd v. *Mardon* [1976] QB 801

Excel Securities plc v. *Masood* [10 June 2009] Manchester Mercantile Court

Field v. *Leeds City Council* (2000) 32 HLR 619

Fiona Trust & Holding Corp. v. *Privalov* [2007] 4 All ER 951, 956–7

About the IBA Arbitration Committee

Established as a Committee of the International Bar Association's Legal Practice Division, which focusses on the laws, practice and procedures relating to the arbitration of transnational disputes, the Arbitration Committee currently has over 2,600 members from 115 countries, and membership is increasing steadily.

Through its publications and conferences, the Committee seeks to share information about international arbitration, promote its use and improve its effectiveness. The Committee has published several sets of rules and guidelines, which have become widely accepted by the arbitration community as an expression of arbitration best practices, such as the IBA Rules on the Taking of Evidence in International Arbitration, as revised in 2010, the IBA Guidelines on Conflicts of Interest in International Arbitration, which are currently under revision, and the IBA Guidelines on Drafting Arbitration Agreements. The Committee also publishes a newsletter twice a year and organises conferences, seminars and training sessions around the globe.

The Committee maintains standing subcommittees and, as appropriate, establishes task forces to address specific issues.

At the time of the issuance of these Guidelines the Committee has – in addition to its Task Force on Counsel Conduct – three subcommittees, namely, the Investment Treaty Arbitration Subcommittee, the Conflicts of Interest Subcommittee and the Young Arbitration Practitioners Subcommittee.

The Guidelines

The IBA Arbitration Committee established the Task Force on Counsel Conduct in International Arbitration (the 'Task Force') in 2008.

The mandate of the Task Force was to focus on issues of counsel conduct and party representation in international arbitration that are subject to, or informed by, diverse and potentially conflicting rules and norms. As an initial enquiry, the Task Force undertook to determine whether such differing norms and practices may undermine the fundamental fairness and integrity of international arbitral proceedings, and whether international guidelines on party representation in international arbitration may assist parties, counsel and arbitrators. In 2010, the Task Force commissioned a survey (the 'Survey') in order to examine these issues. Respondents to the Survey expressed support for the development of international guidelines for party representation.

The Task Force proposed draft guidelines to the IBA Arbitration Committee's officers in October 2012.

The Committee then reviewed the draft guidelines and consulted with experienced arbitration practitioners, arbitrators and arbitral institutions. The draft guidelines were then submitted to all members of the IBA Arbitration Committee for consideration. Unlike in domestic judicial settings, in which counsel are familiar with, and subject, to, a single set of professional conduct rules, party representatives in international arbitration may be subject to diverse and potentially conflicting bodies of domestic rules and norms. The range of rules and norms applicable to the representation of parties in international arbitration may include those of the party representative's home jurisdiction, the arbitral seat, and the place where hearings physically take place. The Survey revealed a high degree of uncertainty among respondents regarding what rules govern party representation in international arbitration. The potential for confusion may be aggravated when individual counsel working collectively, either within a firm or through a co-counsel relationship, are themselves admitted to practise in multiple jurisdictions that have conflicting rules and norms.

In addition to the potential for uncertainty, rules and norms developed for domestic judicial litigation may be ill-adapted to international arbitral proceedings.

Indeed, specialised practices and procedures have been developed in international arbitration to accommodate the legal and cultural differences among participants and the complex, multinational nature of the disputes. Domestic professional conduct rules and norms, by contrast, are developed to apply in specific legal cultures consistent with established national procedures.

The IBA Guidelines on Party Representation in International Arbitration (the 'Guidelines') are inspired by the principle that party representatives should act with integrity and honesty and should not engage in activities designed to produce unnecessary delay or expense, including tactics aimed at obstructing the arbitration proceedings.

As with the International Principles on Conduct for the Legal Profession, adopted by the IBA on 28 May 2011, the Guidelines are not intended to displace otherwise applicable mandatory laws, professional or disciplinary rules, or agreed arbitration rules that may be relevant or applicable to matters of party representation. They are also not intended to vest arbitral tribunals with powers otherwise reserved to bars or other professional bodies.

The use of the term 'guidelines' rather than 'rules' is intended to highlight their contractual nature. The parties may thus adopt the Guidelines or a portion thereof by agreement. Arbitral tribunals may also apply the Guidelines in their discretion, subject to any applicable mandatory rules, if they determine that they have the authority to do so.

The Guidelines are not intended to limit the flexibility that is inherent in, and a considerable advantage of, international arbitration, and parties and arbitral tribunals may adapt them to the particular circumstances of each arbitration.

DISCUSSION

History

[P – 1] The Guidelines were launched in 2013 and form part of the IBA family of Guides and Rules for the conduct of international arbitration – *IBA Rules on the Taking of Evidence in International Arbitration* (2010)[1] (the '**IBA Rules**') and *IBA Guidelines on Conflicts of Interest in International Arbitration* (2014)[2] (the '**IBA Guidelines on Conflicts**') being the others.

[P – 2] In his keynote address to the 2012 ICCA Congress, Sundaresh Menon[3] called for greater regulation in arbitration. He proposed as a *'relatively straightforward and minimally invasive first step ... to develop a code of conduct and practice to guide international arbitrators and international arbitration counsel'*.

[P – 3] That call was not new. The IBA had previously published the IBA International Code of Ethics (1956, updated 1988). In the 2001 Goff Lecture, Johnny Veeder QC noted the fact that practitioners would hail from different cultures 'does not mean that international practitioners are pirates sailing under no national flag; it means only that on the high seas, navigators need more than a coastal chart'. In 2009 Cyrus Benson published a Checklist of Ethical Standards for Counsel in International Arbitration, and in 2010 The Hague Principles on Ethical Standards for Counsel appearing before International Courts and Tribunals were published. At the 2010 ICCA Congress, Doak Bishop had called for a code of conduct and warned of complacency. He and Margrete Stevens offered the Rio Code[4] in the following year, which drew heavily on the 1988 IBA International Code of Ethics and the 2006 Code of

---

[1] See P. Ashford, *The IBA Rules on the Taking of Evidence in International Arbitration: A Guide* (Cambridge University Press, 2013) (*'Guide to the Rules'*).
[2] A Guide by the author will follow.   [3] Then Chief Justice designate for Singapore.
[4] The 2010 Congress was held in Rio de Janeiro.

Conduct for European Lawyers of the CCBE.[5] It was a good start but was not challenging, comprising, as it did, mainly truisms. The Rio Code has largely fallen by the wayside – not surprising, as the authors themselves called upon the ICCA or the IBA to draft a code. Finally, the IBA itself published the IBA International Principles of Conduct of the Legal Profession in 2011 which have largely been replaced/fallen into disuse in light of the Guidelines.

[P – 4] The IBA responded to the call. Indeed, it had already started. In 2008 the IBA established a 'Task Force on Counsel Conduct in International Arbitration'.[6] In 2010 the Task Force commissioned a survey[7] and in October 2012 the Task Force reported with a draft to the IBA Arbitration Committee's officers who, in turn, consulted some practitioners and institutions. Three months later the draft Guidelines were circulated to members,

---

[5] The CCBE Code expressly applies to arbitration (Article 4.5) and hence a lawyer subject to the Code must (a) comply with the rules of conduct applied by the tribunal (Article 4.1); (b) have due regard to the fair conduct of the proceedings (Article 4.2); (c) whilst maintaining due courtesy and respect towards the tribunal, defend the interests of the client honourably and fearlessly without regard to the lawyer's own interests or to any consequences for himself (Article 4.3); and (d) never knowingly give false or misleading information to the tribunal (Article 4.4). The CCBE Code is designed to mitigate the effects of EU Directive 98/5/EC, Article 6.1 of which states: 'Irrespective of the rules of professional conduct to which he is subject in his home Member State, a lawyer practicing under his home country professional title shall be subject to the same rules of professional conduct as lawyers practicing under the relevant professional title of the host Member State in respect of all activities he pursues in its territory.' This appears to embody double deontology: if an English lawyer conducts an arbitration in Paris he may be subject to both English and French regulation. Whether the same applies to the English lawyer acting in a London-seated arbitration who meets a witness in Paris is less clear. The answer probably lies in the Directive referring to practising on a permanent basis, so meeting a witness or even conducting a reference in another Member State would not be caught, but there is little guidance.

[6] It may well be significant that seven of the 23 members hailed from North America and included some of the more prominent members.

[7] A member of the Task Force, Cyrus Benson, comments: 'An extensive and widely circulated survey was conducted, the results of which demonstrated that many participants in international arbitration are uncertain about what rules or sets of rules govern the conduct of party representatives ... A high percentage of those responding to the survey expressed a desire for guidance in this area ...' (Cyrus Benson, 'The IBA Guidelines on Party Representation: an Important Step in Overcoming the Taboo of Ethics in International Arbitration', *Les Cahiers de l'Arbitrage/Paris Journal of International Arbitration*, (2014), 47–57).

inviting comments in some three weeks.[8] There was scathing criticism[9] led by the then ASA President, Michael Schneider. This resulted in some changes: 'shall' became 'should' and other minor textual changes, and weeks later the Guidelines were adopted by the IBA Council.[10]

What the alternatives were

[P – 5] One option would have been to leave matters of counsel conduct to the inherent power of each tribunal without seeking to establish norms of behaviour. On an *ad hoc* basis, tribunals could determine what powers they have and how best any such powers should be exercised. No doubt the fallback would have been that, by entrusting the dispute to the tribunal, and the process for doing so, the parties had presumptively entrusted the tribunal with wide-ranging powers concerning process. Tribunals, in all probability, have the power to combat 'run-of-the-mill' (if there is such a thing) abuse and obstruction by appropriate measures so as to preserve the integrity of the process. The old maxim of 'hard cases make bad law' would arise in this event. There will be well-publicised (or gossiped) instances of outrageous behaviour that justify the need for sanctions for misconduct.

[P – 6] Another route would be to 'legislate' by the route of institutional rules. At the time of writing, only the LCIA has done so, and its Rules are discussed below.

[P – 7] The third option is internationally accepted guidance or rules that can be adopted as and when required. That is the option taken by the IBA with the Guidelines.

---

[8] This timescale has been forcefully criticised.

[9] This continued after adoption: see e.g. Michael Schneider's September 2013 Presidential Message: 'Yet another opportunity to waste time and money on procedural skirmishes: The IBA Guidelines on Party Representation.'

[10] This difficult 'birth' of the Guidelines is significant in understanding the acceptance or otherwise of the Guidelines. There remain calls for a radical rethink. It is not the function or purpose of this Guide to continue the call for a rethink or to endorse the Guidelines as a whole. The Guidelines exist, for better or worse, and this Guide aims to accompany the reader through them. Difficulties and inconsistencies are highlighted for that purpose.

[P – 8] The rationale for the Guidelines is said to be, in part, 'educational',[11] but they go beyond what many would perceive as global minimum standards: in part to combat 'guerrilla tactics', but the guerrilla will often accuse his opponent first to deflect attention away from himself – that is the true behaviour of the guerrilla. One thing that is near certain is that the guerrilla will adapt and find ways around any attempt at regulation.

[P – 9] One of the further reasons to have a single standard reflected in the Guidelines is to avoid the so-called 'double deontology'. To define terms (as most people meeting the phrase for the first time admit to not understanding it): deontology[12] is, in philosophy, a group of ethical theories that place special emphasis on the relationship between duty and the morality of human actions.[13] In deontological ethics an action is considered morally good because of some characteristic of the action itself, not because the product of the action is good. Deontological ethics holds that at least some acts are morally obligatory regardless of their consequences. So, in essence, deontology is, in this context, the set of ethical rules that bind a lawyer (or the rules of the relevant bar or law society). Double deontology is being subject to two or more potentially conflicting sets of rules. This may be because the lawyer is called to two different bars or is a member of two different law societies; or because, being a member of a bar or law society, the lawyer is also subject to the ethical

---

[11] Especially, rather patronisingly, of 'less developed nations' where local rules of the bar 'are not to the same standard' – see Alexis Mourre and Eduardo Zuleta, 'The IBA Guidelines on Party Representation in International Arbitration', Dispute Resolution International, 7:2 (November 2013), 135.

[12] The term *deontology* is derived from the Greek *deon*, 'duty', and *logos*, 'science'. The early developer was Immanuel Kant, a renowned eighteenth century Prussian philosopher. Kant's theory was that nothing was good without qualification: every action is neutral until some outside force qualifies it under some code or structure. Deontology was the system he devised for establishing what was good and what was bad. He reasoned that there was no universal deontology and that every group, or, in theory, every individual, could have its (or his) own deontology.

[13] By contrast, teleological ethics (also called consequentialist ethics or consequentialism) holds that the basic standard of morality is precisely the value of what an action brings into being. Deontological theories have been termed formalistic, because their central principle lies in the conformity of an action to some rule or law.

rules prevailing at a different place where he practises; for example, at the seat.[14]

[P – 10] The spectre of double deontology is, however, a false prophet. The tribunal is not concerned – or, at least, ought not to be – with professional ethics, regulation or discipline. They are, however, concerned with a fair process and determination. It should not be thought that by raising the spectre of double deontology the tribunal is the forum for ethical matters to be resolved, for that is the preserve of national courts, law societies and bars.

[P – 11] It could be said that the Guidelines simply add to the problem rather than being part of the solution. The attempt to legislate creates the potential for disputes over the precise terms and an expectation of behaviours that might have been tolerated or overlooked absent the Guidelines. Furthermore, the tribunal's role is to determine the substantive dispute in an impartial and independent manner and to safeguard the integrity of the process. Involvement in counsel behaviours risks distraction from the primary task and may jeopardise independence and neutrality (or at least the perception of independence ad neutrality). The qualities that a tribunal have to determine the substantive dispute may be ill-suited to investigation into counsel conduct.

An introduction

[P – 12] The Preamble to the Guidelines is no more than an introduction. In contrast, the Preamble to the IBA Rules contains a substantive set of principles that governs the general application and interpretation of the IBA Rules. The IBA Guidelines on Conflicts has no Preamble; rather it has an Introduction that is more of a narrative introduction, owing more to the style of the Guidelines than the IBA Rules.

---

[14] Double deontology is less of a problem within the United States because a lawyer must be licensed in every state in which he practises. Furthermore, the US system has a number of facets that limit the potential for problems: highly regulated reciprocal bar admissions; the differing standards all derive from one source – the ABA Model Rules; there is a common system of common law and legal tradition; and most functions can be performed under one licence.

[P – 13] At the outset it must be emphasised that the Guidelines seek to balance different legal traditions in the context of a healthy debate as to whether the conduct of counsel should be regulated so as to level the playing field between different cultures and practices. As a consequence of the balance that is sought to be struck by the Guidelines they will always be vulnerable to attack as being incomplete, vague or favouring common law or civil law traditions (although nobody really contends for the latter). This is inevitable and should not be seen as a weakness in the Guidelines. The key objective of the Guidelines, as is evident from the preamble, is that counsel "should act with integrity and honesty and should not engage in activities designed to produce unnecessary delay or expense, including tactics aimed at obstructing the arbitration proceedings." The objective is uncontroversial and ought to be widely accepted.

Rationale

[P – 14] The rationale for the Guidelines being guidelines rather than rules is intended, apparently, to "highlight their contractual nature." This is, at best, confusing. One might have thought that rules would be something that the parties, by contract, have adopted; whereas guidelines are guidance that the parties are, strictly, not obligated to comply with, and which hence have less affinity with a contractual relationship. The consequence is said to be that the "parties may thus adopt the Guidelines or a portion thereof by agreement", but precisely the same words appear in Preamble 2 to the IBA Rules, so that is hardly persuasive. The statement that "Arbitral tribunals may also apply the Guidelines in their discretion, subject to any applicable mandatory rules, if they determine that they have the authority to do so" is true but hardly takes the debate any further: it rather begs the question of authority. Absent consent, it is difficult to immediately see where the authority of the tribunal might derive from, especially with regard to Party Representatives rather than as regards the Party itself.

[P – 15] The concluding words of the Preamble, of flexibility and adapting the Guidelines to the particular circumstances of the reference, find near identical words in Preamble 2 to the IBA Rules.

Integrity and honesty

[P – 16] The Preamble states that the taking of evidence shall be conducted with "integrity and honesty". It is not clear why the phrase 'good faith' was not used.[15] Integrity and honesty would seem to amount to much the same thing as 'good faith' – a term used by the IBA Rules (although note that Guideline 27 refers to the good faith of the Party Representative in the context of the tribunal dealing with issues of misconduct, but it does so without imposing the obligation in the first place).[16]

---

[15] There is a respected school of thought that contends that there is a duty to arbitrate in good faith – in turn derived from the general principle that contractual duties must be performed in good faith.

[16] If it is right that integrity and honesty amounts to much the same thing as good faith, the common law has some guidance. Contracts of insurance are regarded as being of the 'utmost good faith', and partnership agreements are likewise viewed as contracts of good faith. In the context of an insurance contract, Lord Mansfield CJ said as long ago as 1766: *'The governing principle is applicable to all contracts and dealings. Good faith forbids either party by concealing what he privately knows, to draw the other into a bargain, from his ignorance of that fact, and his believing the contrary. But either party may be innocently silent, as to grounds open to both, to exercise their judgment upon.'* Carter v. Boehm (1766) 3 Burr 1905, 1910

Nevertheless, in English law, unlike many civil systems, there is no principle of good faith of general application. As Bingham LJ said:

'In many civil law systems, and perhaps in most legal systems outside the common law world, the law of obligations recognises and enforces an overriding principle that in making and carrying out contracts parties should act in good faith. This does not simply mean that they should not deceive each other, a principle which any legal system must recognise; its effect is perhaps most aptly conveyed by such metaphorical colloquialisms as "playing fair", "coming clean" or "putting one's cards face upwards on the table". It is in essence a principle of fair and open dealing ... ': Interfoto Picture Library v. Stiletto Visual Programmes [1989] 1 QB 433, 439

Good faith is recognised in the United States where the Restatement (Second) of Contracts requires that 'every contract imposes on each party a duty of good faith and fair dealing in its performance and enforcement'. Even in the civil law jurisdictions of Western Europe there are very considerable differences in the significance of 'good faith' and the uses to which the doctrine is put within each legal system. In some systems, good faith has provided a basis for pre-contractual grounds for relief or compensation (notably as regards duties of disclosure and information and breaking off from negotiations); the addition of 'supplementary' obligations to those expressly provided for by contract or legislation; the control of unfair contracts; the toughening of sanctions for deliberate breaches of contract; the control of the exercise of a Party's contractual rights; and relief on account of supervening circumstances or the substantively unfair nature of the contract as a whole.

Accepting that 'good faith' must mean something, what lessons can be derived from English case law as to the meaning of the phrase? In one case it was interpreted as the 'observance of reasonable commercial standards of fair dealing': Berkley *Community Villages* v. *Pullen* [2007] EWHC 1130 (Ch); in another that a contractual right could only be exercised for a 'genuine commercial reason': *Paragon Finance* v. *Plender* [2005] 1 WLR

[P – 17] Although many commentators consider good faith to be an implicit duty in arbitration, the IBA Rules did not contain an express requirement of good faith until the 2010 revisions and the Guidelines contain no express duty (although, as mentioned above, there is the reference in Guideline 27). Neither the UNCITRAL Model Law nor most of the sets of well-known institutional arbitral rules includes an express obligation to arbitrate in good faith. Two notable exceptions are Article 15.6 of the Swiss Rules, providing that '[a]ll participants in the proceedings shall act in accordance with the requirements of good faith', and, to a lesser degree, Rule 34(3) ICSID Arbitration Rules, providing that '[t]he parties shall cooperate with the Tribunal in the production of the evidence'. The duty to arbitrate in good faith is generally considered to be derived from and to be an incident of the contractual obligation to arbitrate.

Good faith?

[P – 18] Whilst there is, therefore, no express reference in the Guidelines to a duty of good faith, in many instances the IBA Rules will be adopted or the tribunal will use them as guidance. This may result in both "integrity and honesty" and 'good faith' as Preamble 3 to the IBA Rules provides: 'The taking of evidence shall be conducted on the principles that each Party shall act in good faith…' and see also Article 9.7 of the IBA Rules. Article 9.7 provides that if the arbitral tribunal determines that a Party has failed to conduct itself in good faith in the taking of evidence, the arbitral tribunal may, in addition to any other measures available under the Rules, take such failure into account in the allocation of the costs of the arbitration. Despite the slight variation in wording, ('act' in

3412 and, finally, that it must be exercised 'honestly' with no 'ulterior motive': *Central Estates (Belgravia) Ltd* v. *Woolgar* [1972] 1 Q.B. 48.

Of all the interpretations of 'good faith' it is suggested that the 'observance of reasonable commercial standards of fair dealing' may be a useful yardstick against which integrity and honesty can be measured – such an interpretation would fit into the preamble and would not do any violence to the language. More importantly, it would remove some of the more emotive challenges to the phrase. For example, it is suggested that it is consistent with that interpretation of the duty not to be under an obligation to volunteer information or documents that detract from your own case and to otherwise advance the case in the interests of the client provided that nobody is misled either positively or by silence.

Preamble 3 and 'conduct itself' in Article 9.7), both fairly plainly refer to the same thing. Article 9.7 appears to elevate the duty of good faith from an aspiration to a concrete obligation, the failure to comply with which can be visited by sanctions (also the territory of the Guidelines).[17] The sanctions under the IBA Rules are against a Party rather than the Party Representative, but equally the sanctions under the Guidelines, whilst primarily directed to the Party Representative, can be directed to the Party. As appears from the Committee Comments to Guidelines 1–3, a *'Party Representative, acting within the authority granted to it, acts on behalf of the Party whom he or she represents. It follows therefore that an obligation or duty bearing on a Party Representative is an obligation or duty of the represented Party, who may ultimately bear the consequences of the misconduct of its Representative.'*

[P – 19] Using the tribunal's discretion on the allocation of costs to encourage good behaviour during the course of the arbitration is a mechanism that other arbitral bodies have also introduced. For example, in its *Guidelines for Arbitrators Concerning Exchanges of Information*,[18] the ICDR guideline 8(b) provides that in the event that any Party fails to comply with an order for information exchange, the tribunal may draw adverse inferences and may take such failure into account in allocating costs.

[P – 20] Similarly, in the ICC Commission Report, *Controlling Time and Costs in Arbitration*,[19] the ICC Commission states at para. 82 that, 'The allocation of costs can be a useful tool to encourage efficient behaviour and discourage unreasonable behaviour'. That report continues to give examples of unreasonable behaviour, including, 'excessive document requests, excessive legal argument,

---

[17] Article 9.7 is not restricted to the costs of the taking of evidence itself (the purview of the Rules), but potentially encompasses the entire costs of the arbitration. As always, however, the Rules are limited in their effect by the so-called "General Rules" or any mandatory applicable law (Article 1.1). It seems an omission in the Guidelines to match sanctions available against parties under the IBA Rules with sanctions against Party Representatives under the Guidelines.

[18] Available at www.icdr.org.

[19] Available at www.iccwbo.org/Advocacy-Codes-and-Rules/Document-centre/2012/ICC-Arbitration-Commission-Report-on-Techniques-for-Controlling-Time-and-Costs-in-Arbitration/ (accessed 12 October 2015).

excessive cross-examination, dilatory tactics, exaggerated claims, failure to comply with procedural orders, unjustified applications for interim relief, and unjustified failure to comply with the procedural timetable'.

Matters not addressed

[P – 21] The Guidelines are fairly comprehensive, but not completely so. Perhaps the most obvious omissions are:

- courtesy and respect;
- identification of adverse authority;[20]
- submissions of fact not supported by the evidential record;
- the treatment of improperly obtained evidence;[21]
- undertakings by counsel;
- conflicts of interest between Party and Party Representative;
- confidentiality and privilege issues (including the admissibility of settlement negotiations conducted without prejudice);[22]
- the ability to withdraw/cease to act;
- to be reasonably available;
- whether it is proper to interview more than one witness at a time; and
- which witnesses can and cannot be approached.

[P – 22] This list is, of course, by no means comprehensive and is not a criticism. It can readily be anticipated that some issues were simply too difficult to reach a consensus upon, and furthermore, the Guidelines could not conceivably address every issue that might arise. Equally, some matters – such as fees and marketing – are ones that the IBA should not trespass upon, these being the province of national bars and law societies.

---

[20] See e.g. para. 708 of the (English) Bar Code of Conduct: 'A barrister when conducting proceedings in Court ... must ensure that the Court is informed of all relevant decisions and legislative provisions of which he is aware whether the effect is favourable or unfavourable towards the contention for which he argues.'

[21] This could have complemented IBA Rules Art. 9(2)(b).

[22] There is a general but not universal consensus that such negotiations are not admissible. This is a particular issue in possible sanctions against Party Representatives who may be impeded from disclosing all the matters they may wish to defend themselves.

LCIA Rules

[P – 23] No doubt in part influenced by the Guidelines, the LCIA consulted upon and included in the new 2014 Rules (the LCIA Arbitration Rules 2014 – the '**LCIA Rules**'), rules addressing counsel conduct – the LCIA is the first and, at the time of writing, only institution to do so. The basic structure of the LCIA Rules is set out below and reference is made in the following discussions on the Guidelines to the LCIA Rules to compare and contrast the provisions in the Guidelines with the provisions of the LCIA Rules.

[P – 24] The LCIA Rules set out principles to be followed but do not require submission by the Party Representative to the standards as a condition of counsel appearing before the tribunal. The LCIA Rules are structured quite differently to the Guidelines. In particular, the sanctions under the LCIA Rules are plainly against counsel only, whereas under the Guidelines sanctions can be against the Party (specifically, costs and adverse inferences). So, whilst the behaviours required under the LCIA Rules and the Guidelines have much in common, they depart fundamentally when it comes to sanctions. Under the Guidelines, the Party is responsible for the acts and omissions of his agent, the Party Representative: see the Committee Comments to Guidelines 1 – 3.

[P – 25] The relevant provisions of the LCIA Rules are set out in Appendix 1.

[P – 26] Article 18.1 provides that any party may be represented by one or more[23] legal representatives (although not apparently thereby excluding no legally qualified representatives[24]) appearing by name (this appears to indicate that specific individuals as well as firms must be named) before the tribunal. The word 'may' makes clear that it is a right and not an obligation to be represented.

---

[23] This is not intended to mean that every paralegal should be named. The lead lawyers in a firm will be named and the others will be bound as the sub-agent of the named lead lawyers.

[24] The 1998 LCIA Rules referred to 'legal practitioners or other representatives' and was replaced by 'legal representatives'. This appears to be an attempt to exclude non-lawyer representatives, but according to Rémy Gerbay, Lisa Richman, et al. Arbitrating under the 2014 LCIA Rules, this is a reference to the representative legally representing the Party. If so, this could have been expressed more clearly.

[P – 27] Article 18.2 provides that until the tribunal's formation, the LCIA Registrar, and after formation, the tribunal, may request from any Party: (i) written proof of the authority of any legal representative designated in its Request or Response; and (ii) written confirmation of the names and addresses of all of its legal representatives. This is clearly designed to ensure that any conflict issues (both with individuals and firms) are flushed out at an early stage. It can be readily contemplated that tribunals will at an early stage (perhaps the first procedural meeting) seek confirmation of all legal representatives.

[P – 28] Article 18.3 provides that, following the tribunal's formation, any intended change by a Party to its legal representatives[25] shall be notified promptly in writing to all other parties, the tribunal and the LCIA Registrar; and any such intended change shall only take effect subject to the approval of the tribunal.

[P – 29] The combined effect of Articles 18.2 and 18.3 is to police the identity of legal representatives and ensure that guerrilla tactics are not used to 'parachute in' counsel who has a conflict with a tribunal member and thereby disrupt, at the very least, the arbitration. The key feature is that the intended change does not take effect unless and until approved. That is a much smoother mechanism than the Guidelines approach in Guidelines 5 and 6, which puts the onus on the Party Representative not to accept appointments that would result in conflict (Guideline 5) and then empowers the tribunal to take remedial steps (Guideline 6): by then the problem has arisen and an attempt is being made to bolt the stable door after the horse has gone.

[P – 30] Article 18.4 provides that the tribunal may withhold approval of any intended change to a Party's legal representatives where such change could compromise the composition of the tribunal or the finality of any award (on the grounds of possible conflict or other like impediment). In deciding whether to grant or withhold such approval, the tribunal shall have regard to: (i) the principle that

---

[25] It is arguable that this does not extend to a change of personnel as in-house counsel, as they are not a 'representative' of the Party, but, I suggest, it is wise to notify any such changes in any event if that in-house counsel has a role in the arbitration. The same applies if an individual moves firms.

a Party may be represented by a legal representative of its choice,[26] (ii) the stage which the arbitration has reached,[27] (iii) the efficiency resulting from maintaining the composition of the tribunal[28] and any likely wasted costs or loss of time resulting from such change.[29] Again, this is a sensible route of addressing the issues before they arise – namely, considering whether or not to approve a change in legal representative rather than, under the Guidelines, have a change that is then attacked. In general terms, a change should normally be accommodated save in exceptional circumstances.

[P – 31] Article 18.5 provides that parties have an obligation to ensure that each of their individual legal representatives appearing before the tribunal have agreed to comply with the general guidelines contained in the Annex to the LCIA Rules, and a Party represents that the legal representative has agreed to such compliance. This appears to acknowledge that the route to police the conduct of representatives is through the Party rather than directly to the representative. The position is certainly not clear and the LCIA can be forgiven for opting for the certain route, although it might have been nice to see the direct route contemplated as at least an option if the tribunal found it did have a direct authority. The adherence by the parties to the LCIA Rules is mandatory and does not require an opt-in – in contrast to the Guidelines. It follows from the obligation on the Party to ensure that its representative complies with the provisions of the Annex that the tribunal would have power to sanction the Party for failing to ensure compliance.

[P – 32] Article 18.6 provides that on a complaint by one Party against another Party's legal representative (or of a complaint by

---

[26] See the discussion under Guidelines 26 and 27. The Party seeking change has no burden to show that it is expedient to change the counsel team – the right is not an absolute right – although refusal of a change must be based on recognised and limited exceptions, e.g. conflict of interest.

[27] This is effectively an analysis of the benefit to the Party of having counsel of its choice and the detriment of having to change any member(s) of the tribunal. Plainly, the earlier the change, the more persuasive the former will be; the later the change, the more persuasive the latter.

[28] This is much the same as the previous factor, and the comments in the immediately preceding footnote apply.

[29] A replacement does not imply that the process has to start again. The appointment of a replacement member of the tribunal can be expedited. In general terms, the procedural aspects are unlikely to need to be repeated, whilst an evidentiary hearing would need to be.

the tribunal upon its own initiative), the tribunal may decide, after consulting the parties and granting that legal representative a reasonable opportunity to answer the complaint, whether or not the legal representative has violated the general guidelines. If such violation is found, the tribunal may order any or all of: (i) a written reprimand; (ii) a written caution as to future conduct; and (iii) any other measure necessary to fulfil the general duties, so as to (a) act fairly and impartially, (b) grant a reasonable opportunity to be heard, (c) avoid unnecessary delay and expense and (d) provide a fair, efficient and expeditious resolution. The identity of the complainant is likely to be an area of particular controversy. In some instances, it can only be the tribunal who can raise the issue of misconduct; e.g. improper *ex parte* communications with the tribunal. It does not follow that the tribunal has to be the complainant; indeed, it will be rare that the tribunal acts as 'prosecutor', especially when it is the principal witness.

Definitions

Terms in the IBA Guidelines on Party Representation in International Arbitration

'Arbitral Tribunal' or 'Tribunal' means a sole Arbitrator or a panel of Arbitrators in the arbitration;

'Arbitrator' means an arbitrator in the arbitration;

'Document' means a writing, communication, picture, drawing, program or data of any kind, whether recorded or maintained on paper or by electronic, audio, visual or any other means;

'Domestic Bar' or 'Bar' means the national or local authority or authorities responsible for the regulation of the professional conduct of lawyers;

'Evidence' means documentary evidence and written and oral testimony;

'Ex Parte Communications' means oral or written communications between a Party representative and an Arbitrator or prospective Arbitrator without the presence or knowledge of the opposing Party or Parties;

'Expert' means a person or organisation appearing before an Arbitral Tribunal to provide expert analysis and opinion on specific issues determined by a Party or by the Arbitral Tribunal;

'Expert Report' means a written statement by an Expert;

'Guidelines' mean these IBA Guidelines on Party Representation in International Arbitration, as they may be revised or amended from time to time;

'Knowingly' means with actual knowledge of the fact in question;

'Misconduct' means a breach of the present Guidelines or any other conduct that the Arbitral Tribunal determines to be contrary to the duties of a Party Representative;

'Party' means a party to the arbitration;

'Party-Nominated Arbitrator' means an Arbitrator who is nominated or appointed by one or more Parties;

'Party Representative' or 'Representative' means any person, including a Party's employee, who appears in an arbitration on behalf of a Party and makes submissions, arguments or representations to the Arbitral Tribunal on behalf of such Party, other than in the capacity as a Witness or Expert, and whether or not legally qualified or admitted to a Domestic Bar;

'Presiding Arbitrator' means an arbitrator who is either a sole Arbitrator or the chairperson of the Arbitral Tribunal;

'Request to Produce' means a written request by a Party that another Party produce Documents;

'Witness' means a person appearing before an Arbitral Tribunal to provide testimony of fact;

'Witness Statement' means a written statement by a Witness recording testimony.

DISCUSSION

[D – 1] The definitions are, in the most part, all fairly obvious and most experienced practitioners should cope well without the benefit of them.

[D – 2] Nevertheless, they are valuable to put the point beyond argument and provide clarity and certainty. Regrettably, the definitions are only partially consistent with the definitions in the IBA Rules. The wide definition of "Document" is to be expected and is the same as in the IBA Rules. The Guidelines use the alternative definition of "Tribunal" as well as "Arbitral Tribunal" and conclude with the additional words "in the arbitration", which would appear to add nothing.

[D – 3] The IBA Rules have separate definitions of 'Party Appointed Expert' and 'Tribunal Appointed Expert', whereas the Guidelines have a single definition of "Expert" and the Guidelines provide that the Expert is to "provide expert analysis and opinion" whereas the Rules provide simply that the expert is to 'report'. Finally, the Rules define a 'Witness Statement' as 'a written statement of testimony by a witness of fact', whereas the Guidelines define it as "a written statement by a Witness recording testimony". There is no explanation as to why there should be these differences, and they are to be regretted. It would have made sense for there to be a consistency of definition across the family of IBA Rules and Guidelines.[1]

[D – 4] The definition of Expert might raise an eyebrow by including an organisation as well as an individual. Expert evidence is a professional opinion that an individual can hold and express. It is much more difficult conceptually for an organisation to hold an opinion (in the metaphysical sense) and, to the extent that an organisation can have an opinion (being a collection of transient individuals), for it to hold a single opinion. Even an individual expert will probably be unlikely to hold a view that, say, the value of an asset is X. He is more likely to hold the view that a fair value is between Y and Z, perhaps with X being the average value in the range; or that the value is X with a margin of +/- Y%. If an organisation employs a number of individuals, it is likely that they will not hold identical opinions – hence the range of opinions will be greater in an organisation than with any one individual.

[D – 5] Therefore, whilst the Guidelines contemplate an organisation giving expert testimony, this is best avoided, and the opinion of a single expert – albeit a member of an organisation – should be adduced. The possible exception is that of standards published by respected organisations, whether for e.g. accounting standards and conventions or building standards or methods. It can be readily contemplated that the tribunal may be directed to those standards and indeed that the tribunal might accept such standards, but it is a strange concept to talk of such organisations and the standards that they promulgate "appearing before" the tribunal.

[D – 6] An issue can arise with the status of in-house counsel, who can, of course, appear for the Party. The question arises whether they are representing the company or are a part of the company. If the

---

[1] There is no definition section in the IBA Guidelines on Conflicts.

latter, this could mean that they are not bound by the obligations of the 'legal representative' under the LCIA Rules, but would be bound as a Party Representative as the definition in the Guidelines extends to employees of the Party.

[D – 7] The definition of "Misconduct" is a breach of the Guidelines or any other conduct that the tribunal determines to be contrary to the duties of a Party Representative. This creates an impossible position. It is highly unlikely that tribunals will take up valuable time and effort in Procedural Order No. 1 in further defining what constitutes Misconduct. If that is correct, it means that the tribunal may retrospectively determine whether or not conduct amounts to Misconduct. That raises issues of due process with the potential of a Party Representative being 'convicted' of Misconduct without being aware that what was being done/omitted was Misconduct in the first place. Tribunals would be well advised only to pursue Misconduct that is not specifically outlawed by the Guidelines in very clear cases (i.e. where there would be universal acceptance that the conduct was wrongful – such as criminal conduct).

[D – 8] "Party Representative" is widely defined and includes, as would be anticipated, lawyers but also non-lawyers – indeed anyone by whom the Party wishes to be represented. That this will include persons not subject to any code of ethics is a reason for the existence of the Guidelines, although it cannot be seriously contended that this is <u>the</u> reason for their existence. The reality is that most Party Representatives are lawyers and it is their (mis)conduct that they are largely aimed at, rather than the relatively few non-lawyers.

[D – 9] The definition of "Request to Produce" is the same as under the IBA Rules.

[D – 10] The definition of "Witness Statement" is slightly unusual in referring to its "recording" testimony. When made, it is not really "recording" testimony, and the word might be thought more consistent with a statement recording oral testimony that had been given. It might have been preferable for the Guidelines to adopt the IBA Rules definition: 'a written statement of testimony by a witness of fact'. Again, quite why there is not consistency between the IBA family of documents is unclear and to be regretted.

[D – 11] Although not a defined term, the Guidelines generally use the word "should" rather than "shall". Apparently, earlier drafts generally included the word "shall". The change was due in large part to the criticisms of the ASA, led by Michael Schneider. The criticism focussed on the Guidelines being guidelines.

[D – 12] The counterargument is that 'shall' implies a mandatory obligation, whereas 'should' is a permissive or advisory obligation. The argument runs that there can be no Misconduct if there is a breach of a permissive or advisory obligation as you cannot breach a permissive or advisory obligation. This is illusory logic: for example, Guideline 9 provides that: "A Party Representative should not make any knowingly false submission of fact to the Arbitral Tribunal." Is it seriously to be contended that a false submission of fact is not Misconduct merely because there was no breach of a mandatory obligation as the obligation was merely advisory and the Guidelines are a licence to lie with impunity? Construed as a whole code or document, it is quite plain that that behaviour would be Misconduct.

[D – 13] As mentioned above, the following additional definitions are used here:

"counsel" means a (usually legally qualified) representative who represents or appears in an arbitration on behalf of a client (who is a Party), but it is used to refer to counsel (who is otherwise known in the Guidelines as a Party Representative) otherwise then in the context of the Guidelines;

"IBA Rules" means the IBA Rules on the Taking of Evidence in International Arbitration (2010);[2]

"IBA Guidelines on Conflicts". means the IBA Guidelines on Conflicts of Interest in International Arbitration (2014);[3]

"LCIA Rules" means the LCIA Arbitration Rules 2014.

[D – 14] Quotations from the Guidelines are indicated by double inverted commas, "and", whereas quotations from other materials are indicated by single inverted commas, 'and'.

---

[2] See P. Ashford, *Guide to the Rules*.   [3] A Guide by the author will follow.

Application of Guidelines

1. The Guidelines shall apply where and to the extent that the Parties have so agreed, or the Arbitral Tribunal, after consultation with the Parties, wishes to rely upon them after having determined that it has the authority to rule on matters of Party representation to ensure the integrity and fairness of the arbitral proceedings.
2. In the event of any dispute regarding the meaning of the Guidelines, the Arbitral Tribunal should interpret them in accordance with their overall purpose and in the manner most appropriate for the particular arbitration.
3. The Guidelines are not intended to displace otherwise applicable mandatory laws, professional or disciplinary rules, or agreed arbitration rules, in matters of Party representation. The Guidelines are also not intended to derogate from the arbitration agreement or to undermine either a Party representative's primary duty of loyalty to the party whom he or she represents or a Party representative's paramount obligation to present such Party's case to the Arbitral Tribunal.

IBA COMMITTEE COMMENTS

Comments to Guidelines 1–3

As explained in the Preamble, the Parties and Arbitral Tribunals may benefit from guidance in matters of Party Representation, in particular in order to address instances where differing norms and expectations may threaten the integrity and fairness of the arbitral proceedings.

By virtue of these Guidelines, Arbitral Tribunals need not, in dealing with such issues, and subject to applicable mandatory laws, be limited by a choice of law rule or private international law analysis to choosing among national or domestic professional conduct rules. Instead, these Guidelines offer an approach designed to account for the multi-faceted nature of international arbitral proceedings.

These Guidelines shall apply where and to the extent that the Parties have so agreed. Parties may adopt these Guidelines, in whole or in part, in their arbitration agreement or at any time subsequently.

An Arbitral Tribunal may also apply, or draw inspiration from, the Guidelines, after having determined that it has the authority to rule on matters of Party representation in order to ensure the integrity and fairness of the arbitral proceedings. Before making such determination, the Arbitral Tribunal should give the Parties an opportunity to express their views.

These Guidelines do not state whether Arbitral Tribunals have the authority to rule on matters of Party representation and to apply the Guidelines in the absence of an agreement by the Parties to that effect. The Guidelines neither recognise nor exclude the existence of such authority. It remains for the Tribunal to make a determination as to whether it has the authority to rule on matters of Party representation and to apply the Guidelines.

A Party Representative, acting within the authority granted to it, acts on behalf of the Party whom he or she represents. It follows therefore that an obligation or duty bearing on a Party Representative is an obligation or duty of the represented Party, who may ultimately bear the consequences of the misconduct of its Representative.

DISCUSSION

Application

[1–3 – 1] The first scenario where the Guidelines apply is where the Parties have agreed that they should do so. Note that, although they legislate over the conduct of the Party Representative, there is no need or requirement that the Party Representative himself agrees to submit to the Guidelines. This is consistent with the overarching context of the Guidelines that they are an extension of the agreement to arbitrate (originally a bilateral agreement between the Parties and latterly, it is generally understood to be typically, a tripartite agreement between the Parties and the tribunal), although there is considerable academic debate as to whether it is the status of the tribunal *per se* that gives rise to duties and obligations.[1]

Tribunal Authority

[1–3 – 2] The alternative scenario is that the Guidelines apply where the tribunal, firstly, determines that it has 'authority' to rule on Party representation and, secondly, that it determines that it wishes to rely upon the Guidelines, having consulted the Parties.

[1–3 – 3] The second limb can be dispensed with relatively quickly. If the tribunal reaches that stage of passing the first limb (i.e. the Parties have not agreed to adopt the Guidelines but that the tribunal has found that it has authority to rule on matters of Party representation) it will be grateful for such guidance as exists and the Guidelines, carrying the authority of the IBA, will, as with other IBA publications, command great respect. It is difficult to envisage a tribunal not having regard to the Guidelines in these circumstances. The first limb is, however, more problematic.

[1–3 – 4] If the tribunal has 'authority' over matters of Party representation[2] that authority (or jurisdiction) must derive from something. From where does any such authority derive? The fact that this question has to be posed exposes the flaw in the Guidelines: absent consent few tribunals will have the courage to apply the Guidelines in any substantive way.

---

[1] But see the following discussion.
[2] It is a popular position that tribunals have an inherent power to preserve the integrity of the proceedings by taking measures against disruptive counsel. According to the Swiss Arbitration Association, 'under most if not all frequently used arbitration rules arbitrators have, expressly or by implication, the powers to ensure the "fundamental fairness and integrity" of the proceedings. If they do not always make adequate use of such powers this would seem to be essentially a question of arbitration practice and arbitrator awareness rather than a lack of rules or guidance.' 2014 ASA Report on the Guidelines.

[1–3 – 5] There is only one sensible answer to that question: the agreement to arbitrate.[3] As mentioned above, the arbitration agreement was originally a bilateral agreement between the Parties and latterly is generally understood to be a tripartite agreement between the Parties and the tribunal (although the 'status' debate – i.e. that jurisdiction derives from the status of the tribunal – remains but it is probably a distinction without a difference).[4]

[1–3 – 6] As Sir Nicholas Browne-Wilkinson VC said in *K/s Norjarl A/s* v. *Hyundai Heavy Industries Co. Ltd*[5]:

I find it impossible to divorce the contractual and status considerations: in truth the arbitrator's rights and duties flow from the conjunction of those two elements.

The arbitration agreement is a bilateral contract between the parties to the main contract. On appointment, the arbitrator becomes a third party to that arbitration agreement, which becomes a trilateral contract: see Compagnie Europeene de Cereals SA v Tradax Export [1986] 2 Lloyd's Rep. 301. Under that trilateral contract, the arbitrator undertakes his quasi-judicial functions in consideration of the parties agreeing to pay him remuneration. By accepting appointment, the arbitrator assumes the status of a quasi-judicial adjudicator, together with all the duties and disabilities inherent in that status.[6]

[1–3 – 7] The arbitration agreement is the only instrument governing the Parties' relationship with the tribunal. To the extent that any authority over Party Representatives exists, it must, presumably, derive from the agreement to arbitrate, but, as is often pointed out, the Party Representative is not a party to the agreement to arbitrate.

[1–3 – 8] By an agreement to arbitrate the Parties submit their dispute to decision by the tribunal. The arbitration agreement invariably says nothing about the process or procedure (save that it may be governed by institutional rules).

[3] There is an alternative, albeit underdeveloped, argument that the jurisdiction derives from Article 18 of the Model Law: 'The parties shall be treated with equality and each party shall be given a full opportunity of presenting his case.' This is enacted by §33 Arbitration Act 1996 in England.

[4] Mustill & Boyd being at the forefront of the status argument.   [5] [1992] Q.B. 863.

[6] At page 884 and see Leggatt at page 531: 'I doubt whether analysis of an arbitrator's position in terms of contract will ordinarily yield a different result from analysis in terms of status.' See also *Jivraj* v. *Hashwani* [2009] EWHC 1364.

[1–3 – 9] A tribunal has an obligation to adopt suitable procedures for the circumstances of the particular reference. Thus if the reference turns on a single issue of law it may be inappropriate to have extensive document production and witnesses; rather, written submissions may be sufficient.

[1–3 – 10] The suitable procedures so adopted will also avoid unnecessary delay and expense. In the example above, the written submissions may be considerably quicker and cheaper than the alternative. Of course, institutional rules will invariably confer on the tribunal a broad discretion to make directions as the tribunal sees fit.[7]

[1–3 – 11] Absent institutional rules, the Parties do not expressly bestow the tribunal with any powers relating to process or procedure but there is undoubtedly an implied agreement and it is at this point that the status argument probably amounts to much the same thing as the contractual analysis. The arbitration agreement will define those claims that can and cannot be arbitrated, as stated by Lord Hoffmann in *Fiona Trust & Holding Corp.* v. *Privalov:*[8]

Arbitration is consensual. It depends upon the intention of the parties as expressed in their agreement. Only the agreement can tell you what kind of disputes they intended to submit to arbitration. But the meaning which parties intended to express by the words which they used will be affected by the commercial background and the reader's understanding of the purpose for which the agreement was made. Businessmen in particular are assumed to have entered into agreements to achieve some rational commercial purpose and an understanding of this purpose will influence the way in which one interprets their language ... If one accepts that [consensual dispute resolution outside of the national courts] is the purpose of an arbitration clause, its construction must be influenced by whether the parties, as rational businessmen, were likely to have intended that only some of the questions arising out of their relationship were to be submitted to arbitration and others were to be decided by national courts ... If, as appears to be generally accepted, there is no rational basis upon which businessmen would be likely to wish to have questions of the validity or enforceability of the contract decided by one tribunal and questions about its performance decided by another, one would need to find very clear language before deciding that they must have had such an intention.

---

[7] See e.g. ICC Rules (2012) Article 24; LCIA Rules Article 14.
[8] [2007] 4 All ER 951, 956–7.

[1–3 – 12] This logic can, and should, be extended to bestowing on the tribunal the implied power over the Parties to determine process and procedure so as to ensure the integrity and fairness of the reference (whether as an incident to the arbitration agreement or as a consequence of status). Disputes and differences between the Parties as to whether, when and to what extent there should be, for example, document production are no different, in principle, to disputes and differences over the substantive dispute – if the Parties cannot agree, the tribunal must decide. As an implied term of the agreement to arbitrate it is a part of the agreement to arbitrate and affects and applies to both the Parties and the tribunal.

[1–3 – 13] The question that then arises is whether it is a necessary incident of the power to control process and procedure, as described, that that power includes power to rule on matters affecting the Parties' Representatives just as much as it is to order a Party to, for example, produce documents.

[1–3 – 14] As discussed above, the LCIA Rules approach the authority over counsel by placing the obligation on the Party to 'ensure' that counsel adhere to the required behaviours and the Party also represents that the counsel has so agreed as a condition of his appearance. Note that counsel makes no representation and gives no warranty. As mentioned above, the application of the Guidelines depends on agreement or the tribunal finding that it has the required authority.

[1–3 – 15] Working from first principles, and as mentioned above, any power over the Party Representative (as opposed to the Party) must derive from the agreement to arbitrate; that agreement is initially bilateral, and becomes trilateral when the dispute arises and the tribunal is formed.

[1–3 – 16] That trilateral agreement is usually formed by a Request for Arbitration and Answer/Response in institutional references (or a notice to concur in *ad hoc* references). The Request and Answer/Response will usually be submitted by Party Representatives. They will act as agent for their clients, the Parties – who will be the (disclosed) principal for whom the Party Representative is agent.

[1–3 – 17] As a matter of orthodox agency law, the agent is not, generally, liable on a contract made for a disclosed principal. The reason for this, where it is the case, is that however objectively construed the trilateral contract so formed is between the principal, the Party and the other Party and the tribunal:

There is no doubt whatever as to the general rule as regards an agent, that where an agent contracts as agent for a principal, the contract is the contract of the principal and not that of the agent; and, prima facie, at common law the only person who may be sued is the principal and the only person who can be sued is the principal.[9]

[1–3 – 18] An agent can, however, be liable to a third party without being able to sue (in this analogy, the Party Representative is liable to, i.e. subject to the discipline of, the tribunal, and to a (very) limited extent may be liable to the other Party even though it stands to gain no benefit from the reference – other than being remunerated). This liability is on the basis that a collateral contract can be inferred on the basis that the agent (the Party Representative), in return for the third parties (the other Party and the tribunal) dealing with its principal (the Party), undertakes personal liability on the main contract (i.e. the now-trilateral agreement to arbitrate).

[1–3 – 19] There is, however, nothing to stop the agent (the Party Representative) entering into a contract on the basis that it will, itself, be liable to perform it, as well as the principal (the Party).[10] The modern trend is to recognise such liabilities, for example, under collateral contracts (the consideration for which is the entering into the main contract with the principal) an agent may warrant his authority. A specialised application of the warranty of authority is that given by counsel who issues process in litigation (or arbitration). In general, counsel warrants that he has been authorised by a client that exists.[11] There are clear limits on the warranty – it does not extend to the name of the client being correct; nor that the client is

---

[9] *Montgomerie* v. *UK Mutual SS Assn Ltd* [1891] 1 QB 370, 371. See also *Paquin* v. *Beauclerk* [1906] AC 148. UNIDROIT Principles (2004) Art. 2.2.3 and Restatement of Agency, Third §6.01 both appear to have the same starting point.

[10] *International Ry* v. *Niagara Parks Commission* [1941] AC 328, 342.

[11] *Nelson* v. *Nelson* [1997] 1 WLR 233.

solvent; nor that the claim is valid or even arguable – but the basic, and limited, warranty is well recognised.

[1–3 – 20] In litigation there is no need for the warranty of authority to extend to submitting to the discipline of the court as that is usually well covered by an inherent power of state courts to control counsel appearing before it. It follows that the warranty has never been analysed in that way in litigation. The reasoning of counsel's liability has recently been extended: a lawyer acting for the purchaser of land has been found to warrant to prospective mortgage lenders.[12] Bearing in mind the general principles that an agent can be liable with the principal, it is suggested that it is not a large leap of reasoning for the Party Representative to owe duties to the tribunal and hence for the tribunal to be able to enforce those duties.

[1–3 – 21] The above analysis is based on contractual duties of the agent (counsel), principal (Party) and third party (tribunal – and, perhaps, other Party). In tort, the agent is generally personally liable where loss, damage or injury is caused to the third party by a wrongful act or omission of the agent just as if he were acting on his own behalf.[13] It will be no defence for the agent to say he was acting under instructions of his principal.[14]

[1–3 – 22] In torts connected to the contract it is clear that the agent may also be liable to the third party in deceit.[15] Equally, it is clear that the agent for one Party may owe duties to the other Party: the most obvious situation being negligent misstatement or representation. However, this analysis only goes so far – it may give a third party a cause of action but it is unlikely to give a third party a power to exercise a disciplinary function.[16]

[1–3 – 23] It is therefore clear that, in a variety of situations, an agent (a Party Representative) may owe enforceable duties to a third party (the tribunal) both in contract (and tort, to the extent relevant). So

---

[12] *Excel Securities plc* v. *Masood* [June 10, 2009] Manchester Mercantile Court.
[13] Restatement of Agency, Third §7.01: 'An agent is subject to liability to a third party harmed by the agent's tortious conduct …'
[14] *Bennett* v. *Bayes* (1860) 5 H&N 391.
[15] *Standard Chartered Bank* v. *Pakistan National Shipping Corp* [2003] 1 AC 959.
[16] See e.g. *Esso Petroleum Co. Ltd* v. *Mardon* [1976] QB 801.

much is consistent with existing authority. Those principles can (and, perhaps, ought readily to) be extended to afford the tribunal a contractual jurisdiction over Party Representatives who act as agent when the trilateral arbitration agreement is formed for the tribunal to adjudicate on the particular dispute referred to it. The principles do not so easily apply to counsel who may join the legal team after the arbitration agreement is formed. However, on analysis, the notification of additional (or replacement) counsel can be seen as a variation of the original agreement (whereby, in consideration of being allowed to appear, the new or additional Party Representative adopts the duties and obligations as Party Representative).[17]

[1–3 – 24] The logic for having such a jurisdiction can be tested by supposing that a Party Representative returns to the hearing room at night to copy his opponent's private and privileged notes. It would be surprising if the tribunal were impotent and unable to act. Equally, it would be fair, reasonable and proper for the tribunal to have jurisdiction to, at the very least, order the delivery up or destruction of such copies and to sanction counsel for such behaviour. How far that jurisdiction extends – for example, whether it extends to removing counsel from the arbitration – is another matter, and is discussed under Guidelines 26 and 27. That there is a jurisdiction is, I suggest, clear. Whether it derives from status or contract/agency is not immediately important, but the contract/agency argument is more principles than the status argument.

[1–3 – 25] Furthermore, whether and how such jurisdiction should be exercised is entirely another matter as it may be incompatible with the tribunal's duty to determine the parties' dispute and may impact upon the impartiality of the tribunal, or at least might raise the appearance of partiality.[18]

---

[17] See e.g. *Bak* v. *MCL Financial Group Inc.* 88 Cal. Rptr. 3d 800 (Cal. App. 2009), where a tribunal ordered counsel to pay $7,500 as a sanction for copying privileged documents as 'by voluntarily appearing' counsel 'subjected himself to the jurisdiction of [the tribunal] and was subject to its rulings'.

[18] There is undoubtedly authority that holds that tribunals do not have the jurisdiction argued for here and it is recognised that the proposition is novel. Authorities holding that the tribunal does not have jurisdiction include: *InterChem Asia 2000 Pte Ltd* v. *Oceana Petrochemicals AG* 373 F.Supp.2d 340 (SDNY 2005) (where an award of legal costs of $70,000 was made against counsel for 'peculiar and extremely harmful dealing with

[1–3 – 26] Guideline 2 provides, uncontroversially, that the Guidelines are to be interpreted in accordance with their overall purpose and, perhaps more controversially, in accordance with the most appropriate manner for the particular arbitration.

[1–3 – 27] The purpose of the Guidelines is not expressly stated, but presumably it is a reference to the words in the Preamble: "party representatives should act with integrity and honesty and should not engage in activities designed to produce unnecessary delay or expense." The advantage of the preponderance of 'soft law' in arbitration is to achieve a consistency of approach such that international arbitration can be predictable. If the Guidelines are to be interpreted differently in arbitration 'A' from an interpretation in arbitration 'B', the advantages of certainty in this arena of soft law disappear. It is a different matter entirely for there to be a consistency of approach or interpretation and yet the application to be fact or reference sensitive. To this extent the Guidelines can, and should, be adapted to the particular circumstances of the reference. That, I suggest, is the correct approach.

[1–3 – 28] Guideline 3 records that the Guidelines, being guidelines, do not displace laws, professional rules or applicable institutional rules. Although perhaps obvious, it does no harm to state the obvious for the avoidance of any doubt but the Party Representative must show the mandatory law(s) that is/are applicable to him. Firstly, the rules of the local bar or law society where the Party Representative practices will apply (although they may have a carve-out for international arbitration). Secondly, if the lawyer is admitted in more than one jurisdiction, more than one set of rules may apply. Thirdly, some rules relating to counsel conduct may apply under the mandatory laws of the seat. Finally, there may be universal codes of conduct or guidelines such as the CCBE Code of Conduct for European Lawyers (2006). It is a difficult problem with no easy answer. The

documents in the case' was set aside as it 'exceeded the arbitrator's authority'); *CBC Oppenheimer Corp.* v. *Friedman* 2002 WL 244820 (Cal. App.) (where an award holding counsel jointly and severally liable for costs of $700,000 for filing a frivolous claim without factual foundation was set aside as 'representation … at the arbitration cannot be construed as his agreement to become a party to the arbitration agreement'; and see *MCR of America Inc.* v. *Greene* 811 A.2d 331 (Md. App. 2002).

best attempt to date is the ICDR International Arbitration Rules, which provide that 'when the parties, their counsel or their documents would be subject under applicable law to different rules, the Tribunal should, to the extent possible, apply the same rule to all parties, giving preference to the rule that provides the highest level of protection'.[19]

[1–3 – 29] The statement that the Guidelines do not derogate from the agreement to arbitrate is, perhaps, obvious (unless it is agreed that the Guidelines be formally adopted, but even then the Guidelines are highly unlikely to conflict with the agreement to arbitrate itself).

[1–3 – 30] Greater meat is to be found in recording that the Party Representative's primary duty of loyalty is owed to the client. Many of the Guidelines impose duties that may conflict with the obligation of undivided loyalty owed to the client. For example, Guideline 13 imposes an obligation not to make a Request for Document production so as to cause delay. Delay is often something that is the friend of one Party and the enemy of the other Party. Assume the Party instructs the Party Representative that it is to seek delay at every opportunity. The duty of loyalty obliges the Party Representative to do so, if necessary, by making an extensive Document production Request (having warned of the costs consequences of doing so and the adverse impression made on the tribunal). In an adversarial system the tribunal will rule so as to ensure that fair play is observed and not oblige the opposing Party to produce non-relevant and non-material documents. It will be a defence to most allegations of Misconduct that the Party Representative was acting on instructions and consistent with the duty of loyalty owed to the Party instructing him.

[1–3 – 31] Guideline 3 also records the Party Representative's paramount duty to present the Party's case to the tribunal. This is a basic obligation and uncontroversial. An advocate is obliged to present

---

[19] ICDR Rules (2014) Article 22 and see also JAMS Efficiency Guidelines for the Pre-Hearing Phase of International Arbitrations (2011): '… in JAMS international arbitrations when the parties, their counsel or their documents would be subject to different rules or other obligations with respect to things such as privilege, privacy or professional ethics, the arbitrator applies the same rule to both sides where possible giving preference to the rule that provides the highest level of protection.'

the Party's case without fear or favour – that obligation is at the heart of most justice systems. Again this aspect will conflict with other Guidelines, or at least, for example, the Committee Comments to Guidelines 9–11 which provide that *'With respect to legal submissions to the Tribunal, a Party Representative may argue any construction of a law, a contract, a treaty or any authority that he or she believes is reasonable.'* It follows from this that the Party Representative should not make a subjectively unreasonable submission (admittedly derived from the Comments rather than the Guidelines themselves). It is difficult to reconcile this with the 'paramount' duty to present the Party's case to the tribunal. It is not, nor should it be, the Party's case only if and to the extent that the Party Representative thinks it is reasonable. This plainly demonstrates that the Committee's Comment to Guidelines 9–11 may conflict with the duty of loyalty.[20]

[1–3 – 32] The Guidance also records that the Party Representative, whilst acting within the authority granted to it, acts on behalf of the Party whom he or she (or it) represents. So far this is uncontroversial. The Guidance continues: "It follows therefore that an obligation or duty bearing on a Party Representative is an obligation or duty of the represented Party". This reflects that the Party Representative is the agent and the Party is the principal, hence the obligation of the agent is the obligation of the principal if, and only if, the agent has, on a proper construction of the agreement to arbitrate the particular dispute with the tribunal, undertaken those obligations. Note that the Guidance must be read as if the word 'also' were included so that it reads: "It follows therefore that an obligation or duty bearing on a Party Representative is <u>also</u> an obligation or duty of the represented Party" (emphasis added).

[1–3 – 33] As discussed above, the party to the agreement to arbitrate is the Party itself and not its representative. It follows that the obligations or duties on a Party also bind the Party Representative, who acts as the Party's agent – and not the other way around. It is ultimately the Party who will bear the consequences of the

---

[20] The Committee Comments aim to prevent subjectively unreasonable arguments. Most Bar Standards will have an objective standard of something akin to 'properly arguable'. See the discussion on Guidelines 9–11.

misconduct of its representative. For example, assume parties A and B are in a reference and X represents A. X is guilty of misconduct, which the tribunal considers should be reflected by an order (or award) of costs.

[1–3 – 34] The tribunal could either: (a) make an order in favour of B against A, recording that it arises from X's misconduct; or (b) make an order against X. The order against A could even be an award and would be readily enforceable. An order against X might have, if the reasoning above is not accepted, questionable jurisdiction and might also be unenforceable. Unless X paid the order voluntarily, the practical utility might be questionable and B may well prefer an order against A for these very reasons – indeed, it might be worse off by having an order against X.

[1–3 – 35] The tribunal ought, it is suggested, to either (a) make an order against A expressing the hope (and expectation) that X will indemnify A – this leaves B with an enforceable order (or award) and the ultimate burden might well fall on X (as the tribunal intended); (b) make an order against A and X jointly; or (c) make an order against X with a remedy over against A if X does not pay – effectively making A the guarantor of X's liability. The first option is, however, preferable, as it does not involve the jurisdictional issues of making an order against X in the first place.[21]

---

[21] It is not infrequently that tribunals purport to make orders against representatives/counsel e.g. on disputed Redfern Schedule items directing that counsel search and certify that there are no responsive documents. The jurisdiction to do so is, at best, unclear. Even if the logic at [1–3 – 18] above is accepted, the Party Representative's personal liability on the agreement to arbitrate may well not extend to being directed as to how that agreement should be performed.

Party representation

4. Party Representatives should identify themselves to the other Party or Parties and the Arbitral Tribunal at the earliest opportunity. A Party should promptly inform the Arbitral Tribunal and the other Party or Parties of any change in such representation.
5. Once the Arbitral Tribunal has been constituted, a person should not accept representation of a Party in the arbitration when a relationship exists between the person and an Arbitrator that would create a conflict of interest, unless none of the Parties objects after proper disclosure.
6. The Arbitral Tribunal may, in case of breach of Guideline 5, take measures appropriate to safeguard the integrity of the proceedings, including the exclusion of the new Party Representative from participating in all or part of the arbitral proceedings.

IBA COMMITTEE COMMENTS

Comments to Guidelines 4–6

Changes in Party representation in the course of the arbitration may, because of conflicts of interest between a newly-appointed Party Representative and one or more of the Arbitrators, threaten the integrity of the proceedings. In such case, the Arbitral Tribunal may, if compelling circumstances so justify, and where it has found that it has the requisite authority, consider excluding the new Representative from participating in all or part of the arbitral proceedings. In assessing whether any such conflict of interest exists, the Arbitral Tribunal may rely on the IBA Guidelines on Conflicts of Interest in International Arbitration.

Before resorting to such measure, it is important that the Arbitral Tribunal give the Parties an opportunity to express their views about the existence of a conflict, the extent of the Tribunal's authority to act in relation to such conflict, and the consequences of the measure the Tribunal is contemplating.

DISCUSSION

Identification

[4–6 – 1] Party Representatives are normally identified in the Request for Arbitration and Answer or Response. These documents are normally submitted before the tribunal is appointed and the tribunal members, when proposed, consider any possible conflict with the Parties and the Party Representatives. If a conflict exists, or circumstances exist that should be declared, the nominated tribunal member will, or certainly should, declare it and will either withdraw, not have his candidature confirmed, or be confirmed. In this way there are rarely conflicts that arise between the tribunal and the (original) Party Representatives unless there has been a non-disclosure or inadequate initial disclosures. The same rigour does not necessarily (or even usually) apply to checking conflicts where there are changes to the Party Representatives (often because the new or additional Party Representatives are not announced to the tribunal or the institution).

[4–6 – 2] The obligation to notify changes is the logical extension of the original basis of identifying Party Representatives. It plainly extends to the entire team and not just to the counsel of record. In the US with a unified profession, this will be less of an issue (although in large cases there will often be more than one firm involved which may, or may not, be revealed).

[4–6 – 3] In the UK the solicitors will usually appear in the Request or Answer but the barrister will not normally be named unless he has settled the pleading and barristers are often not involved at the Request/Answer stage other than in an advisory role. Thus the name and chambers of any barristers involved may not be apparent until a procedural conference, a pleading that they have signed or even appearance at an evidential hearing. For this reason, it is advisable to disclose new members of the legal team/new counsel as soon as is practicable (including naming the full team in the Request/ Answer). This dispels any impression of ambush and enables any issues of possible conflict to be addressed as early as possible.

[4–6 – 4] The concept of giving notice of changes and additions is fundamental to the Guidelines for the behaviour (of potential conflict and other disruption) can only be challenged and policed if the Party Representative is known to exist and his identity is known.

[4–6 – 5] More problematic are the guerrilla tactics of appointing counsel late (or revealing the appointment of counsel appointed some time ago, shortly before a hearing). What has come to be regarded as the archetypal example of this is the ICSID case of *Hrvatska Elektropivreda d.d.* v. *Republic of Slovenia.*[1]

[4–6 – 6] The evil that is addressed by the Guidelines is an appointment of the new Party Representative such as it (in the words of Guideline 5) "would" create a conflict.[2] It is surprising that the test is not the same as that under the IBA Guidelines on Conflicts that refers to an objective standard of a reasonable observer having justifiable doubts as to impartiality or independence. This is all the more so as the Committee Comments state that the tribunal may rely upon the IBA Guidelines on Conflicts. It might be argued that the reference to a conflict is a conflict as defined by the IBA Guidelines on Conflicts and, of course, there is an obvious good sense of consistency.

[4–6 – 7] A further peculiarity, if the Guidelines are to be read with the IBA Guidelines on Conflicts, is that Guideline 5 refers to the possibility that the parties might not object. That is inconsistent with the non-waivable red list under the IBA Guidelines on Conflicts where Party agreement (or non-objection) is not possible and the conflict position is such that one or other of the proposed Party Representative or the tribunal member must, in that event, go (or a change not be approved).

---

[1] ICSID Case No. ARB/05/24, 6 May 2008. Discussed below under Guidelines 26 & 27.
[2] This requirement for an actual conflict is reinforced by the Comments which refer to *'conflicts of interest'* that *'threaten the integrity of the proceedings'*.

[4–6 – 8] The power to exclude is then engaged and the exercise of such power may be considered in "compelling circumstances". In considering the exercise of such a power the tribunal should "give the Parties an opportunity to express their views about the existence of a conflict, the extent of the Tribunal's authority to act in relation to such conflict, and the consequences of the measure the Tribunal is contemplating." There is no mention of consulting or permitting the Party Representative to express any view.[3] The reality is that the Party will make submissions and will do so through, at least, the existing Party Representative. It must be assumed that if the proposed new Party Representative has anything to say it will be said through the Party's instruction of the existing Party Representative.

[4–6 – 9] Critics point to the Committee Comments and the need for the tribunal to establish that it has authority. If the Guidelines do not give that authority, what is their purpose? Furthermore, Guideline 6 might prompt a tribunal to act beyond its jurisdiction, which, in turn, would give rise to challenges, delay and potentially an unenforceable award. The answer is simply that this reference to establishing authority is a reference back to the second scenario in Guideline 1.

[4–6 – 10] Article 18.3 of the LCIA Rules provides for a similar but importantly different method of policing changes in Party Representatives. Rather than putting the burden on the Representative not to accept the appointment the LCIA Rules provide that any intended change shall only take effect subject to the approval of the tribunal. This is a preferable route to that in the Guidelines.[4]

---

[3] Note that the Party Representative is consulted if there is an allegation of misconduct against him – see the Committee Comments to Guideline 27.
[4] At the IBA Arbitration Day in Paris, 2014 Klaus Reichert SC suggested that in the Terms of Reference (or first Procedural Order) it be recited, or an order be made, to the following effect: 'The parties agree that any change or addition to a party's legal representation as set out herein after the date of these Terms of Reference must be notified to the other party and the Tribunal forthwith. The parties further agree that, in order to ensure the integrity of the proceedings, the Tribunal may refuse to permit a party's legal representative to appear, where the appearance of such legal representative may otherwise require the recusal of a member of the Tribunal.'

[4–6 – 11] Article 18.4 of the LCIA Rules provides that the tribunal may withhold approval of any intended change to a Party's legal representatives where such change could compromise the composition of the tribunal or the finality of any award (on the grounds of possible conflict or other like impediment). Again, this is a sensible route of addressing the issues before they arise – namely, considering whether or not to approve a change in legal representative rather than, under the Guidelines, have a change that is then attacked.

Communications with Arbitrators

7. Unless agreed otherwise by the Parties, and subject to the exceptions below, a Party Representative should not engage in any Ex Parte Communications with an Arbitrator concerning the arbitration.
8. It is not improper for a Party Representative to have Ex Parte Communications in the following circumstances:
   (a) A Party Representative may communicate with a prospective Party-Nominated Arbitrator to determine his or her expertise, experience, ability, availability, willingness and the existence of potential conflicts of interest.
   (b) A Party Representative may communicate with a prospective or appointed Party-Nominated Arbitrator for the purpose of the selection of the Presiding Arbitrator.
   (c) A Party Representative may, if the Parties are in agreement that such a communication is permissible, communicate with a prospective Presiding Arbitrator to determine his or her expertise, experience, ability, availability, willingness and the existence of potential conflicts of interest.
   (d) While communications with a prospective Party-Nominated Arbitrator or Presiding Arbitrator may include a general description of the dispute, a Party Representative should not seek the views of the prospective Party-Nominated Arbitrator or Presiding Arbitrator on the substance of the dispute.

Comments to Guidelines 7–8

Guidelines 7–8 deal with communications between a Party Representative and an Arbitrator or potential Arbitrator concerning the arbitration.

The Guidelines seek to reflect best international practices and, as such, may depart from potentially diverging domestic arbitration practices that are more restrictive or, to the contrary, permit broader Ex Parte Communications.

Ex Parte Communications, as defined in these Guidelines, may occur only in defined circumstances, and a Party Representative should otherwise refrain from any such communication. The Guidelines do not seek to define when the relevant period begins or ends. Any communication that takes place in the context of, or in relation to, the constitution of the Arbitral Tribunal is covered.

Ex Parte Communications with a prospective Arbitrator (Party-Nominated or Presiding Arbitrator) should be limited to providing a general description of the dispute and obtaining information regarding the suitability of the potential Arbitrator, as described in further detail below. A Party Representative should not take the opportunity to seek the prospective Arbitrator's views on the substance of the dispute.

The following discussion topics are appropriate in pre-appointment communications in order to assess the prospective Arbitrator's expertise, experience, ability, availability, willingness and the existence of potential conflicts of interest:

(a) the prospective Arbitrator's publications, including books, articles and conference papers or engagements;

(b) any activities of the prospective Arbitrator and his or her law firm or organisation within which he or she operates, that may raise justifiable doubts as to the prospective Arbitrator's independence or impartiality;

(c) a description of the general nature of the dispute;

(d) the terms of the arbitration agreement, and in particular any agreement as to the seat, language, applicable law and rules of the arbitration;

(e) the identities of the Parties, Party Representatives, Witnesses, Experts and interested parties; and

(f) the anticipated timetable and general conduct of the proceedings.

Applications to the Arbitral Tribunal without the presence or knowledge of the opposing Party or Parties may be permitted in certain circumstances, if the parties so agreed, or as permitted by applicable law. Such may be the case, in particular, for interim measures.

Finally, a Party Representative may communicate with the Arbitral Tribunal if the other Party or Parties fail to participate in a hearing or proceedings and are not represented.

DISCUSSION

Communications with the tribunal

[7–8 – 1] Guidelines 7 and 8 address *ex parte* communications by a Party Representative (who will typically be a lawyer, but note that they do not have to be) with the tribunal or one of its (putative) members. The Guidelines do not expressly address a Party itself communicating with the tribunal: this is because the Guidelines themselves address the role of Party Representatives and not of the Parties themselves. It does not mean, of course, that Parties can communicate with the tribunal with impunity. The Guidelines assume that Parties are represented. If a Party is not represented, great care should be taken with any *ex parte* communication between the Party itself and the tribunal: a tribunal (or any actual or prospective member) should either insist that these be in writing or, if an *ex parte* meeting cannot be avoided (and it is difficult to envisage many cases where it cannot, beyond the other Party failing to attend a meeting or hearing), a full note or minute of any such meeting is made by the tribunal secretary (if one has been appointed – and, if not, consider whether one should be appointed) or another independent observer. If a Party is represented there should be no need for direct contact by a Party with the tribunal (or a member) and a tribunal (or any actual or prospective member) should resist direct contact (other than in writing) and insist on any communication being made by the Party Representative.

General prohibition and exceptions

[7–8 – 2] Guideline 7 contains a general prohibition and Guideline 8 has exceptions to that general rule. There is further exception in Guideline 7: that the communication must concern the arbitration itself. There is, therefore, no rule against purely social exchanges at, e.g. a cocktail party. Nevertheless, on the basis that justice must not only be done but also be seen to be done, it is unwise for lengthy private[1] exchanges between a Party Representative and an Arbitrator. This is not to say that, e.g. in a coffee break, a tribunal member cannot exchange pleasantries with a Party Representative, but this is typically done in a public area and not in a secretive or covert manner.

[7–8 – 3] As might be expected from an IBA publication, the net impression of Guidelines 7 and 8 is that they reflect the generally accepted standards of international conduct. Perhaps surprisingly, *ex parte* applications are relegated to the Comments and are not addressed in the text of the Guidelines. No doubt this is because there is no universal standard concerning *ex parte* interim measures. Undoubtedly, there is a preponderance of opinion that *ex parte* interim measures are inconsistent with the clearly established right of a Party to be heard. This is discussed below.

CIArb guidelines

[7–8 – 4] Guidelines 7 and 8 stand comparison with much of the publication by The Chartered Institute of Arbitrators as *Practice Guideline 16 (The Interviewing of Potential Arbitrators)*. Those guidelines are referred to (so as to avoid confusion with the IBA Guidelines) as the CIArb guidelines. CIArb's guidelines are contained in paragraph 3.1, and hereafter, references to paragraphs are to sub-paragraphs of 3.1. The CIArb guidelines focus more on the practicalities of any communication and refer to the interaction as an interview. The CIArb guidelines cover matters such as a clear

---

[1] That is, other than openly, before or within earshot of the opposing Party. A good rule is to ask the question: 'if the opponent had a transcript of this exchange, would there be any sense of embarrassment?' If the answer is anything other than a resounding 'no' then it should not be happening.

understanding of the basis upon which the interview is to be conducted (CIArb guidelines 1 and 2); that appointment carries no obligation to the appointer beyond selecting a chair and ensuring that Parties' arguments are given a fair hearing (3); that the interviewed potential Arbitrator should be permitted to be accompanied by an assistant to take a note (5); that the interview team should be made known and should normally be led by a senior external lawyer (6); that the interview should be recorded or a detailed note taken (7); and that the mere fact of an interview should not be a ground for challenge (8).

[7–8 – 5] The meat of the CIArb guidelines is to be found in (9) and (10), and these correspond with guidelines 8(a) and (d). CIArb guideline (9) provides that the specific facts or circumstances giving rise to the dispute, the position or arguments of the Parties and the merits of the case, may not be discussed with a potential Arbitrator. CIArb guideline 10 provides that the following can be discussed: the names of the Parties (and any third parties) involved or likely to be involved; the general nature of the dispute; sufficient detail of the 'project' for the interviewer and interviewee to assess the latter's suitability for appointment; the expected timetable; the language, governing law and seat; and the interviewee's experience, expertise and availability.

[7–8 – 6] There is a nuanced difference between the Guidelines permitting a "general description" of the dispute to be raised (albeit without seeking views on the substance of the dispute) and the CIArb guidelines permitting the 'general nature' but not the 'specific facts or circumstances' of the dispute to be discussed. A general description would seem to permit some specific facts or circumstances to be included in a discussion.

[7–8 – 7] What is plain under both the Guidelines and the CIArb guidelines is that any discussion of the merits is not permissible. The potential appointee cannot be asked for his views on a particular issue. In contrast, it is generally permissible to assess the familiarity or knowledge of the law (both governing and arbitration), the nature or type of project or technical process, or other area of dispute (see e.g. CIArb guideline 11).

The approach with the chair/sole

[7–8 – 8] It is common practice that there should be no interviewing of a chair or sole appointee other than by the Parties jointly and, indeed, this is normally done at the Parties' behest by the two Party nominee Arbitrators. They will, however, not normally engage in an interview-type process; rather, they will be familiar with the pool of arbitrators and narrow the field by their own knowledge and expertise.[2]

Non-participating Party

[7–8 – 9] The further exception mentioned in the Comments applies where the other Party fails to participate in a hearing and is not represented. This gives rise to several issues:

[7–8 – 10] Firstly, even if a Party is not actively participating in a reference, written communications should still be addressed to it in order that it can belatedly play such part as it can or is permitted to. There is no excuse for not addressing communications even to the most recalcitrant Party.

[7–8 – 11] Secondly, it is inevitable that if a Party is neither present nor represented at a hearing, oral submissions and other communications will be in that Party's absence and hence technically *ex parte*. In such circumstances, it is advisable to have a transcript or other proper record of what was said.

[7–8 – 12] Thirdly, the language of the Comment might be interpreted as saying that the exception applies (i.e. a Party can make *ex parte* communications) if both the other Party fails to attend <u>and</u> that the Party is not represented. The logical conclusion of this might be that if the defaulting Party is represented and neither the Party Representative nor the Party attends the hearing, then there can be no *ex parte* communications. That, I suggest, is too strict an interpretation. The better interpretation is that it is not an *ex parte* communication if the Party is present either in person or by its Party

---

[2] Any "interview" may be no more than a 'do you fancy chairing an [LCIA] tribunal with us as wingmen?'-type chat.

Representative. The corollary of that proposition is that if neither the Party nor any Party Representative, that it might have engaged, is present at a hearing (having been given due notice), *ex parte* communication is necessary and hence permitted.

Ex parte applications

[7–8 – 13] Whilst the Guidelines themselves do not address *ex parte* applications, the Committee Comments raise the possibility without endorsing it: *'Applications to the Arbitral Tribunal without the presence or knowledge of the opposing Party or Parties may be permitted in certain circumstances, if the parties so agreed, or as permitted by applicable law. Such may be the case, in particular, for interim measures.'*

[7–8 – 14] This Guide is not the place to debate whether *ex parte* applications have a place in arbitration, although the latest incarnation of the Model Law expressly permits *ex parte* applications.[3] It is a

---

[3] Although the current Model Law provides in Article 17: '(1) Unless otherwise agreed by the parties, the arbitral tribunal may, at the request of a party, grant interim measures.' This is expanded by new Articles 17A–17H. Article 17A lays down three conditions for the granting of interim measures: irreparable harm that cannot be adequately compensated for by an award of damages, that harm substantially outweighing any likely damage to the Party required to comply with the measure, and a reasonable possibility that the requesting Party will succeed on the merits. Article 17B provides for orders to be made *ex parte* where necessary with the recipient of the order having the right to request variation or termination of the measure. Once an order has been made, the tribunal must, under Article 17C, give notice to all parties of the request for the interim measure, the application for the preliminary order and any communication between any Party and the tribunal on the subject. The tribunal must then hear any application to modify or set aside the order at the earliest practicable time. A preliminary order expires after twenty days, although the tribunal can issue an interim measure adopting or modifying the order once the respondent has had an opportunity to apply to have it lifted. Preliminary orders bind the parties but cannot be enforced through the courts. National laws enacted on previous versions of the Model Law, e.g. English Arbitration Act 1996, provide, in s. 39, for tribunals to order on a provisional basis any relief that they would have power to grant in a final award such as the payment of money or transfer of property and interim payments on account of the costs of the arbitration. This is, however, only if the parties have conferred that power on the tribunal – which will usually be done by adopting institutional rules, although institutional rules do not generally expressly address *ex parte* applications. It will, in each case, be a matter of construing the agreement to arbitrate (including all relevant laws and rules) whether the power to grant *ex parte* relief is conferred on the tribunal. The principal argument against *ex parte* applications being relied upon is that it does not treat the parties with equality and give them both an opportunity to be heard. In determining issues of provisional relief, tribunals are, in general, not bound by law or precedent that governs a court considering the grant of such relief.

fairly constant theme of modern arbitration practice, rules and legislation to give or recognise the power given to tribunals to make orders for preliminary and interim relief. It is much more controversial whether *ex parte* interim relief can be granted. In many instances, it will be unclear (at best) whether the tribunal has jurisdiction to grant *ex parte* relief. The duty on the Party Representative applying for *ex parte* relief[4] is to ensure, as best it can, that the application is fairly (bearing in mind that the tribunal will be hearing only one Party/side) put to the tribunal.

[7–8 – 15] That involves (a) explaining where the tribunal's jurisdiction derives from and drawing the tribunal's attention to arguments that might be made (and certainly those that have been made) that the tribunal would not have jurisdiction; and (b) when addressing the application threshold requirements (irreparable harm that cannot be adequately compensated for by an award of damages; that harm substantially outweighing any likely damage to the party required to comply with the measure, and a reasonable possibility that the requesting party will succeed on the merits) drawing the tribunal's attention to arguments that might be made (and certainly those that have been made) against any of those requirements and generally defences and arguments that might be made against the applicant. It is generally advisable to exhibit any correspondence where the respondent has set out a defence or argument.

When obligations arise

[7–8 – 16] Finally, the Guidelines do not address when the restrictions apply. Does the obligation commence on the notice of arbitration being served or when the arbitration commences? It would be, at best, unfortunate, if a Party Representative felt able to discuss the merits with a prospective tribunal member simply because the arbitration was to commence the following day. Any discussion of the merits with a prospective arbitrator should be avoided at any time. This applies equally to any stage before the arbitration as it does to such a discussion with an actual tribunal member after the

---

[4] This does not arise under the Guidelines but it is an obligation nevertheless.

arbitration has ended and even if the arbitrator is *functus officio*. If there is a social discussion with someone not perceived as a prospective or potential arbitrator (perhaps because arbitration itself is not contemplated) and material information conveyed, that person should consider himself conflicted from any subsequent appointment.

Submissions to the Arbitral Tribunal

9. A Party Representative should not make any knowingly false submission of fact to the Arbitral Tribunal.

10. In the event that a Party Representative learns that he or she previously made a false submission of fact to the Arbitral Tribunal, the Party Representative should, subject to countervailing considerations of confidentiality and privilege, promptly correct such submission.

11. A Party Representative should not submit Witness or Expert evidence that he or she knows to be false. If a Witness or Expert intends to present or presents evidence that a Party Representative knows or later discovers to be false, such Party Representative should promptly advise the Party whom he or she represents of the necessity of taking remedial measures and of the consequences of failing to do so. Depending upon the circumstances, and subject to countervailing considerations of confidentiality and privilege, the Party Representative should promptly take remedial measures, which may include one or more of the following:
    (a) advise the Witness or Expert to testify truthfully;
    (b) take reasonable steps to deter the Witness or Expert from submitting false evidence;
    (c) urge the Witness or Expert to correct or withdraw the false evidence;
    (d) correct or withdraw the false evidence;
    (e) withdraw as Party Representative if the circumstances so warrant.

IBA COMMITTEE COMMENTS

Comments to Guidelines 9–11

Guidelines 9–11 concern the responsibility of a Party Representative when making submissions and tendering evidence to the Arbitral Tribunal. This principle is sometimes referred to as the duty of candour or honesty owed to the Tribunal.

The Guidelines identify two aspects of the responsibility of a Party Representative: the first relates to submissions of fact made by a Party Representative (Guidelines 9 and 10), and the second concerns the evidence given by a Witness or Expert (Guideline 11).

With respect to submissions to the Arbitral Tribunal, these Guidelines contain two limitations to the principles set out for Party Representatives. First, Guidelines 9 and 10 are restricted to false submissions of fact. Secondly, the Party Representative must have actual knowledge of the false nature of the submission, which may be inferred from the circumstances.

Under Guideline 10, a Party Representative should promptly correct any false submissions of fact previously made to the Tribunal, unless prevented from doing so by countervailing considerations of confidentiality and privilege. Such principle also applies, in case of a change in representation, to a newly-appointed Party Representative who becomes aware that his or her predecessor made a false submission.

With respect to legal submissions to the Tribunal, a Party Representative may argue any construction of a law, a contract, a treaty or any authority that he or she believes is reasonable.

Guideline 11 addresses the presentation of evidence to the Tribunal that a Party Representative knows to be false. A Party Representative should not offer knowingly false evidence or testimony. A Party Representative therefore should not assist a Witness or Expert or seek to influence a Witness or Expert to give false evidence to the Tribunal in oral testimony or written Witness Statements or Expert Reports.

The considerations outlined for Guidelines 9 and 10 apply equally to Guideline 11. Guideline 11 is more specific in terms of the remedial measures that a Party Representative may take in the event that the Witness or Expert intends to present or presents evidence that the Party Representative knows or later discovers to be false. The list of remedial measures provided in Guideline 11 is not exhaustive. Such remedial measures may extend to the Party Representative's withdrawal from the case, if the circumstances so warrant. Guideline 11 acknowledges, by using the term 'may', that certain remedial measures, such as correcting or withdrawing false Witness or Expert evidence may not be compatible with the ethical rules bearing on counsel in some jurisdictions.

DISCUSSION

Not to mislead

[9–11 – 1] The essence of Guidelines 9–11 is that the Party Representative should not mislead the tribunal. In principle, that cannot be an objectionable standpoint.[1]

[9–11 – 2] Guideline 9 addresses the Party Representative knowingly submitting a false fact or factual situation. Whether a Party Representative "knows" a fact to be false is, of course, the key aspect of the Guideline. It is not enough that he believes it to be false: Guideline 9 uses the word "knowingly" and the Committee Comments refer to *'actual knowledge'*. In general terms there are several degrees of knowledge or belief. In ascending order:

(a) a Party Representative may have a hunch, gut feeling or doubts concerning the veracity of the account of events – the Guidelines do not prevent the Representative from submitting that which he does not believe and which is not demonstrably false;

(b) there are documents which cast doubt on (but do not flatly contradict) the account of events or there are inconsistencies in the account of events that give rise to legitimate concerns that the account is false – the Guidelines do not prevent the Representative from submitting that which he does not believe and which is not demonstrably false (but as a matter of good practice he should explore the concerns he has with the client so as to resolve them not only for his own benefit but so that the tribunal can be presented with the best case);

---

[1] Similar sentiments can be found in a variety of Statutes, Bar and Law Society rules: e.g. Singapore Legal Profession Act Cap 161 §56; Hong Kong Code of Conduct for Barristers rule 12.

(c) there are documents which flatly contradict the account of events and for which there is no proper explanation[2] or the account of events changes significantly – at the risk of repetition, the question is whether the Party Representative 'knows' the truth but actively or passively allows the tribunal to be misled. I suggest that whilst he may have a high degree of conviction that one or other scenario is the correct one, we are still in the realms of belief and not knowledge; and

(d) the Party informs the Party Representative that the truth is one account of events but intends to lead evidence to the contrary or tells the Party Representative to ignore, conceal or disregard documents that flatly contradict the evidence to be led without providing any plausible explanation. That amounts to knowledge and would breach the Guideline.

[9–11 – 3] Of course, there may be many variants of the above, but it is hoped that these practical examples assist. These observations are references in the Committee Comments to the Party Representative having *'actual knowledge'* although the Comments continue that this can be *'inferred from the circumstances'*. This creates a quandary – the circumstances may create an inference that the Party Representative ought to have known that what was being submitted was incorrect, but the circumstances will rarely enable or permit a look inside the mind of the Representative. Furthermore, the opening words of the Committee Comments refer to the duty of *'candour or honesty'*: these words – in particular, *'candour'* – could well lower the bar below actual knowledge. It is safer to focus on actual knowledge rather than embark on the more exotic notions of openness extending to a sort of confessional.

Submissions unsupported by the record

[9–11 – 4] The more controversial area is submissions that are not necessarily untrue (in the sense of contrary to the record) but are unsupported by evidence. The Guidelines do not address this, but professional ethics often do: e.g. ABA Model Rules of Professional

---

[2] For example, an unanswered email refers to an agreed variation to a contract having been reached at a meeting but the client denies that that occurred.

Conduct Rule 3.1 and Code of Conduct of the Bar of England and
Wales Articles 704 and 708.[3] The former requires a 'basis in fact'
and the latter a consistency with the client's instructions and a
requirement to be 'properly arguable'.

Correction of earlier false statements

[9–11 – 5] Guideline 10 provides for the correction of a previously
false statement (made innocently) as soon as the Party Representative
becomes aware of the truth – this applies, according to the
Committee Comments, to prior submissions by a predecessor Party
Representative. At first blush this may seem a natural corollary of the
duty not to mislead by a false statement in the first instance. The

---

[3] Rule 3.1: Meritorious Claims & Contentions

A lawyer shall not bring or defend a proceeding, or assert or controvert an issue therein,
unless there is a basis in law and fact for doing so that is not frivolous, which includes a good
faith argument for an extension, modification or reversal of existing law. A lawyer for the
defendant in a criminal proceeding, or the respondent in a proceeding that could result in
incarceration, may nevertheless so defend the proceeding as to require that every element of
the case be established.

Drafting Documents

704. A barrister must not devise facts which will assist in advancing the lay client's case and
must not draft any statement of case, witness statement, affidavit, notice of appeal or other
document containing:

   (a) any statement of fact or contention which is not supported by the lay client or by his
instructions;

   (b) any contention which he does not consider to be properly arguable;

   (c) any allegation of fraud unless he has clear instructions to make such allegation and has
before him reasonably credible material which as it stands establishes a prima facie case
of fraud;

   (d) in the case of a witness statement or affidavit any statement of fact other than the
evidence which in substance according to his instructions the barrister reasonably
believes the witness would give if the evidence contained in the witness statement or
affidavit were being given in oral examination;

provided that nothing in this paragraph shall prevent a barrister drafting a document
containing specific factual statements or contentions included by the barrister subject to
confirmation of their accuracy by the lay client or witness.

Conduct in Court

708. A barrister when conducting proceedings in Court:

   (a) is personally responsible for the conduct and presentation of his case and must exercise
personal judgement upon the substance and purpose of statements made and questions
asked; …

   (f) must not make a submission which he does not consider to be properly arguable.

Guideline makes it clear, however, that confidentiality or privilege may prevent the Party Representative from doing so – and it is difficult to conceive of a situation when the Representative will learn of the truth otherwise than in a confidential or privileged communication, whether because the Party admits that to the Representative or otherwise.[4]

[9–11 – 6] The Party Representative will then ordinarily be prevented by reason of confidentiality and/or privilege, absent the consent of the Party, from informing the tribunal of the truth. The Representative then has a conflict between a duty not to permit the tribunal to proceed on a false premise and the duty of confidence owed to the client. The answer to that conundrum lies in the Party Representative's professional rules and ethics but in many situations the Representative may be able to properly withdraw the offending evidence without necessarily replacing it with the 'truth' – that meets the requirement not to permit the tribunal to proceed on a false basis whilst not breaching confidentiality and privilege. Only rarely will the ultimate sanction of having to withdraw, if the Party does not consent to the false statement being corrected, arise. This final step is consistent with Guideline 11(e).

Submissions on the law

[9–11 – 7] Whilst the Guidelines are silent on submissions of law, the Committee Comments go on to say that the Party Representative may make any submission as to the law, authority, contract or treaty he believes to be reasonable.

[9–11 – 8] Firstly, it is noteworthy that this is a Comment only and not a Guideline.

[9–11 – 9] Secondly, the Comment uses a subjective, rather than an objective, test – albeit that this is consistent with the Bar Code of

---

[4] Other likely situations, for example, a witness saying that something did or did not happen, contrary to the Party's account of events, will be likely only to give rise to a strong belief rather than knowledge. Circumstances can be envisaged where, however, the strength of what is said tips the balance to knowledge, especially if the witness is the only person with knowledge of the matter.

Conduct. The ABA Model Rules of Professional Ethics has an objective standard of there being a basis in fact. The Guidelines approach of a subjective (rather than objective) test is unlikely to give rise to uniform behaviours, which is surely at the heart of the Guidelines.

[9–11 – 10] Thirdly, the language is framed as permissive: the ability to argue what is considered reasonable rather than a prohibition on arguing what is unreasonable. This implies that the Party Representative must satisfy himself of the reasonableness of any argument of submission before making it – it does not mean he believes it to be correct only that it is a reasonable argument. Although a competent Party Representative would no doubt consider the reasonableness of any argument he was to advance, to not argue something, even if it is thought to be unreasonable, may well conflict with the overriding duty to act in the best interests of the client and the "paramount" duty in Guideline 3.

[9–11 – 11] Fourthly, there seems no logical basis why the making of a submission that is not subjectively (as opposed to objectively) reasonable adversely affects, in the words of the Preamble, the "fairness and integrity" of the arbitral process. If it is a poor submission it will be dismissed.

[9–11 – 12] Fifthly, again by reference to the words of the Preamble, there is, I suggest, no inconsistency with making a subjectively unreasonable submission with a duty or objective "not [to] engage in activities designed to produce unnecessary delay or expense". Indeed, it is consistent with a Party's right to be heard. If a submission or argument is not reasonable the tribunal will have little trouble in summarily rejecting it.

Remedial steps

[9–11 – 13] Guideline 11 is really a subset of Guideline 10 (as the Committee Comments make clear) and concerns false testimony. It is unlikely to arise for expert testimony (although, of course, it could). Far more likely is the situation of witnesses of fact giving false evidence. The potential for the Party Representative to make a false submission of fact will usually follow a witness statement or oral testimony, so the comments under Guidelines 9 and 10 apply equally to Guideline 11.

[9–11 – 14] The remedial steps in Guideline 11 are mandatory ("should") in the event of a breach of the Guidelines but the particular remedial steps are prefaced by the word "may include" so the remedial action is not limited to the specific matters mentioned and might take any form that the Party Representative considers appropriate. Guidelines 11 (a)–(c) (to advise, deter and urge) are simply means by which the Party Representative might seek to have the false evidence corrected. Guideline 11 (d), to correct the false evidence, will again engage issues of confidentiality and privilege. In most cases the Representative will not be able to correct without the client's permission.[5] This leaves the nuclear option of Guideline 11 (e), that the Party Representative withdraws from acting for the Party, which, in practice, is the only realistic option if the client insists on misleading the tribunal.

[5] Some commentators advocate the position that privilege should not condone the tribunal being misled and hence the representative is at liberty to correct. Obviously, the laws of privilege will vary depending on the laws to which the representative is subject, but the latter part of Guideline 11 might be redundant if it were that simple. An alternative is just to withdraw the evidence but not replace it.

Information exchange and disclosure

12. When the arbitral proceedings involve or are likely to involve Document production, a Party Representative should inform the client of the need to preserve, so far as reasonably possible, Documents, including electronic Documents that would otherwise be deleted in accordance with a Document retention policy or, in the ordinary course of business, which are potentially relevant to the arbitration.

13. A Party Representative should not make any Request to Produce, or any objection to a Request to Produce, for an improper purpose, such as to harass or cause unnecessary delay.

14. A Party Representative should explain to the Party whom he or she represents the necessity of producing, and potential consequences of failing to produce, any Document that the Party or Parties have undertaken, or been ordered, to produce.

15. A Party Representative should advise the Party whom he or she represents to take, and assist such Party in taking, reasonable steps to ensure that: (i) a reasonable search is made for Documents that a Party has undertaken, or been ordered, to produce; and (ii) all non-privileged, responsive Documents are produced.

16. A Party Representative should not suppress or conceal, or advise a Party to suppress or conceal, Documents that have been requested by another Party or that the Party whom he or she represents has undertaken, or been ordered, to produce.

17. If, during the course of an arbitration, a Party Representative becomes aware of the existence of a Document that should have been produced, but was not produced, such Party

Representative should advise the Party whom he or she represents of the necessity of producing the Document and the consequences of failing to do so.

IBA COMMITTEE COMMENTS

Comments to Guidelines 12–17

The IBA addressed the scope of Document production in the IBA Rules on the Taking of Evidence in International Arbitration (see Articles 3 and 9). Guidelines 12–17 concern the conduct of Party Representatives in connection with Document production.

Party Representatives are often unsure whether and to what extent their respective domestic standards of professional conduct apply to the process of preserving, collecting and producing documents in international arbitration. It is common for Party Representatives in the same arbitration proceeding to apply different standards. For example, one Party Representative may consider him- or her-self obligated to ensure that the Party whom he or she represents undertakes a reasonable search for, and produces, all responsive, non-privileged Documents, while another Party Representative may view Document production as the sole responsibility of the Party whom he or she represents. In these circumstances, the disparity in access to information or evidence may undermine the integrity and fairness of the arbitral proceedings.

The Guidelines are intended to address these difficulties by suggesting standards of conduct in international arbitration. They may not be necessary in cases where Party Representatives share similar expectations with respect to their role in relation to Document production or in cases where Document production is not done or is minimal.

The Guidelines are intended to foster the taking of objectively reasonable steps to preserve, search for and produce Documents that a Party has an obligation to disclose.

Under Guidelines 12–17, a Party Representative should, under the given circumstances, advise the Party whom he or she represents to: (i) identify those persons within the Party's control who might possess Documents potentially relevant to the arbitration, including electronic Documents; (ii) notify such persons of the need to preserve and not destroy any such Documents; and (iii) suspend or otherwise make arrangements to override any Document retention or other policies/practises whereby potentially relevant Documents might be destroyed in the ordinary course of business.

Under Guidelines 12–17, a Party Representative should, under the given circumstances, advise the Party whom he or she represents to, and assist such Party to: (i) put in place a reasonable and proportionate system for collecting and reviewing Documents within the possession of persons within the Party's control in order to identify Documents that are relevant to the arbitration or that have been requested by another Party; and (ii) ensure that the Party Representative is provided with copies of, or access to, all such Documents.

While Article 3 of the IBA Rules on the Taking of Evidence in International Arbitration requires the production of Documents relevant to the case and material to its outcome, Guideline 12 refers only to potentially relevant Documents because its purpose is different: when a Party Representative advises the Party whom he or she represents to preserve evidence, such Party Representative is typically not at that stage in a position to assess materiality, and the test for preserving and collecting Documents therefore should be potential relevance to the case at hand.

Finally, a Party Representative should not make a Request to Produce, or object to a Request to Produce, when such request or objection is only aimed at harassing, obtaining documents for purposes extraneous to the arbitration, or causing unnecessary delay (Guideline 13).

DISCUSSION

Criticisms of document production

[12–17 – 1] Guidelines 12–17 have been subject to particular criticism. The criticism is specifically that they are premised on broad or extensive document production which may be familiar territory for US and other common law jurisdictions – something that is not only unfamiliar to many other jurisdictions but is deeply objectionable. Many users and practitioners would question the premise not least on the basis that arbitration constitutes a genuine alternative to litigation in common law state courts rather than mirroring its processes.

[12–17 – 2] Guideline 12, in particular, is criticised as it is said that (i) document production is already governed by the IBA Rules[1], (ii) it extends document production beyond the IBA Rules, and (iii) although the Guidelines purport only to address ethical conduct, they expand document production obligations.

Preservation

[12–17 – 3] Guideline 12 addresses the duty of the Party Representative to advise on document retention – the so-called 'litigation hold' or 'litigation freeze'.[2] The duty under the Guideline extends to include the preservation of those documents that might be destroyed/deleted under a document retention policy or otherwise. The Committee Comments clarify the extent of the duty by defining the duty as extending to (i) identifying those persons within the Party's control (presumably those employed and agents – the latter including external counsel) who might possess documents potentially relevant to the arbitration, including electronic documents; (ii) notifying such persons of the need to preserve and not destroy any such documents; and (iii) suspending or otherwise making arrangements to override any document retention or other policies/practices whereby potentially relevant documents might be destroyed in the ordinary course of business.

[12–13 – 4] The obligation applies "so far as reasonably possible", so it does not create absolute obligations.[3] Admittedly, what a hardened US litigator might view as reasonable is likely to be quite different from the perception of a civil lawyer from Europe. The answer is that it is not a subjective test but an objective one settled upon, albeit

---

[1] This, in basic terms, is a misplaced concern. The IBA Rules address the scope of document production; the Guidelines address the role and obligations of Party Representatives. The IBA Rules and the Guidelines, quite properly, complement each other.

[2] This is a peculiarly common law concept, and much more of an issue in the US than, say, the UK. It has been criticised as assuming the obligation. That is a little unfair. No obligation can arise unless and until the Parties agree to adopt the Guidelines (and do not, as they could, exclude any particular part of the Guidelines). The basic obligation of not destroying potentially material evidence cannot, at its core, be objectionable. Whilst objection might be taken to the precise language of the Guideline, its purpose is sound.

[3] Note that the reasonableness refers to the obligation to preserve and not to the Party Representative's obligation to advise.

usually retrospectively, by the tribunal. Whilst that puts the Party Representative at risk for taking a view that the tribunal subsequently disagrees with, that is not an unusual risk for Party Representatives – they will make many calls on the reasonableness of their own actions and the duties of the Party they represent.

The onset of the obligation to preserve

[12–13 – 5] The glaring hole in Guideline 12 is when the duty first arises. It seems from the Committee Comments that it is at a relatively early stage – which must be correct, as it refers to being before the materiality of the Documents can be assessed. This does not, however, really assist the debate. The reference in Guideline 12 to "when the arbitral proceedings involve or are likely to involve Document Production" implies, by the use of the definite article, that the arbitral proceedings are on foot or have been commenced (the doubt introduced by the words, "likely to involve", as to whether or not there will be document production is, on the ordinary meaning of the language, designed for an early stage of the arbitration before directions have been made rather than before the arbitration commences). This is logical as the Guidelines are unlikely to be referred to in the agreement to arbitrate, and are likely to be adopted by the parties and the tribunal at the first procedural meeting, and hence they cannot logically apply before adoption (although there is no reason, in principle, why they could not be agreed to apply with retrospective effect).

[12–13 – 6] It would plainly be wrongful for Party Representatives to advise that documents be destroyed the day before commencing the arbitration. The better view is that a Party Representative should considered itself to be under the obligation from the moment that a reference is reasonably foreseeable (see below) and certainly from when the arbitration is commenced – and this is reflected in Guideline 12. That is not to say that an obligation cannot arise at a different time – but it is safer to err on the side of caution.

[12–13 – 7] The practice of the common law courts may assist in determining the onset of the obligation. In most common law courts the concept of a 'litigation freeze' operates to suspend any routine document destruction so as to preserve evidence for the trial or evidentiary hearing. Those that do not observe the 'freeze' are guilty of what in the US is called 'spoilation'. In Australia and the UK the sanctions for spoilation only arise if there is an attempt to pervert the course of justice or the acts would amount to a contempt of court, i.e. the proceedings must be underway: see generally *British American Tobacco Australia Services* v. *Cowell*[4] and *Douglas* v. *Hello.*[5]

[12–13 – 8] In the US the obligation arises when the litigation is 'pending or reasonably foreseeable' – an objective test not susceptible to any gloss; reasonably foreseeable does not require that litigation be imminent or probable: see generally *Micron* v. *Rambus*[6] and *Hynix* v. *Rambus.*[7]

[12–13 – 9] Clearly, when a reference is reasonably foreseeable might be quite different for claimant and respondent Party Representatives. The claimant might know that a reference is likely long before a respondent who might only know of the imminence of the reference when it is actually on foot. A degree of subjective knowledge is, accordingly, likely to be relevant.

Sanction for non-preservation

[12–13 – 10] In the US the *Rambus*[8] decisions make it clear that the ultimate sanction for spoliation in court proceedings is the dismissal of the claim or the striking out of the defence. This ultimate sanction applies were there is (1) bad faith; (2) prejudice to the other party; (3) an evaluation of the degree of (1) and (2); and (4) a finding that no lesser sanction is sufficient.[9] The UK position is that a claim or defence in court proceedings will not be struck out if a fair trial remains possible: *Arrow Nominees Inc.* v. *Blackledge.*[10] A tribunal is very unlikely to have the power to strike out and, in the event that it does, to exercise that power. Clearly, however, if the ultimate

---

[4] [2002] CA (Vic) 6 December 2002.   [5] [2003] EWHC 55 (Ch).
[6] [2011] Supp. 2d. No. 00–792-SLR (D. Del. 2 January 2013).
[7] [2011] 645 F. 3d. 1336 (Fed. Cir. 2011).   [8] Op. cit.
[9] Simply for the facts; the challenge was a technical point on the evidence – see the tribunal dismissing a claim for spoliation without, apparently, applying *Rambus* in *Attia* v. *Audionamix Inc.* 14 Civ 706 SDNY (21 September 2015).
[10] [2001] BCC 591.

sanction is not imposed, adverse inferences can be drawn for the failure to produce relevant and material documents.

Relevant materials

[12–13 – 11] Guideline 12 also makes it clear that the obligation to preserve extends to "potentially relevant" documents. This is plainly wider than the 'relevant and material' test under Article 3 of the IBA Rules. The logic for this is clear: at the early stages of the arbitration before the issues are fully pleaded out the documents that would meet the test of relevance and materiality may not be obvious and hence the obligation is to retain a wider pool until the relevance becomes clear. It might be questioned why the obligation to preserve does not extend to 'potentially relevant and material', but the absence of the materiality test is understandable. The materiality tends to narrow down the relevant document population rather than enlarge it. This is because under the IBA Rules that document must be both relevant and material.[11]

[12–13 – 12] Relevance, in this context, should be given a wide interpretation. It should not be restricted to documents that the Party might wish to rely upon. Clearly if a Party destroys documents that advance its own case it has only itself to blame. The evil that the Guideline is aimed at is the destruction of documents that are adverse to a Party's case or assist the opponent's case[12] and hence the obligation to preserve should specifically focus on adverse documents and the definition of relevance should have a broad compass.

---

[11] E.g. if ten documents go to prove the same point, it might well be that the eleventh, whilst relevant, might not be material to the outcome – as the first ten documents are enough to prove the point.

[12] It might be said that if the obligation arises at or before the commencement of the reference, e.g. the claimant might not know what defence (or counterclaim) might be advanced. Although this is a theoretical problem, it is unlikely that a reference would be commenced without some knowledge of likely defences (whether through pre-reference correspondence or otherwise). If there were a genuinely new defence not foreshadowed then a failure to preserve documents might be excusable. Whilst what will be relevant may be difficult to identify, it is surely easier to identify the larger category of documents that might potentially be relevant.

Improper document requests

[12–13 – 13] Guideline 13, providing that a Request to Produce should not be used for an improper purpose, is an 'apple pie' truism that will cause no controversy; nor will it particularly assist the Party Representatives in framing a proper Request to Produce.[13] It adds little to inform the appropriate standard of behaviour to say that it should not be for an improper purpose, or so as to harass or cause delay. That is not to say that a Request to Produce that causes delay should either be disallowed or would constitute Misconduct. Guideline 13 addresses the purpose of the Request: the purpose should not be to harass or cause delay. If delay is the byproduct of a properly framed Request, that is entirely proper and, perhaps, inevitable.

[12–13 – 14] Tribunals usually have little difficulty with an over-zealous Request to Produce. Requests will be rejected for a variety of reasons, foremost among which is a lack of specificity or other reason linked to Article 3 of the IBA Rules. More helpful would be guidelines to avoid the prolix and unfocussed Request or Requests that are otherwise non-compliant with Article 3 of the IBA Rules. Guideline 13 could easily have been structured around Article 3 of the IBA Rules: e.g. that Requests should not seek documents where the description is insufficient to identify them (c.f. Article 3.3(a)(i)) or that Requests should only be made if they identify why the documents requested are relevant to the case and material to its outcome (c.f. Article 3.3(b)).[14]

---

[13] The genesis of Guideline 13 is fairly transparently US Federal Rules of Civil Procedure Rule 26(G)(I): "...not interposed for any improper purpose such as to harass, cause unnecessary delay, or needlessly increase the cost of litigation; and neither unreasonable nor unduly burdensome or expensive considering the needs of the case, prior discovery in the case, the amount in controversy, and the importance of the issues at stake in the action." This does nothing to lessen the concerns of over-Americanization of the Guidelines, albeit the particular safeguards are laudable.

[14] In practice, tribunals will be well able to police Requests in a Redfern Schedule format especially if the standard format is adapted to include specific columns where the relevance and materiality are required to be completed with specificity (with cross-referencing back to the pleadings – indeed, this should be how well-drafted Redfern schedules are structured in any event – and is something that tribunals should consider insisting upon). Tribunals often comment that the parties know the issues and documents much better than the tribunal will (at least at the time of the document production stage) and the parties must, accordingly,

[12–13 – 16] The 'narrow and specific' under Article 3 of the IBA Rules requirement is one that continues to exercise practitioners and tribunals alike.[15] The issue, for current purposes, will be whether a Request that is denied might be viewed as having been for "an improper purpose". The primary line of defence will be that the purpose must be assessed subjectively, and provided the Request, albeit refused, is subjectively reasonable, that should be the end of the matter. If, however, the Request appears to the tribunal to have been hopeless, they may question whether it can have been thought to have been a reasonable Request or not (i.e. does it fall in the category of Request that no reasonably competent Party Representative could have considered a proper Request?) and hence whether it might have been advanced for "an improper purpose".

[12–13 – 17] In practice, tribunals apply a fairly strict view of identifying a category within a document request, and many requests are denied for a lack of specificity. This should not automatically prompt the further enquiry of whether it is put forward in bad faith. The requesting Party may wish to have disclosure of documents it has difficulty in specifying with any accuracy. This is the more so where it relates to actions in which the requesting Party was not involved. The Party against whom the document production is sought may wish to know precisely what it should search for and to have considerable specificity so as to limit the scope of what has to be given. This is likely to a particularly acute where the Parties (and their Party Representatives) have different (cultural) expectations. One Party may view as harassment what another may view as a legitimate search for the truth. A well-framed request should seek the disclosure of documents that relate to specific issues in the arbitration (and preferably cross-referenced to specific paragraphs in the memorials/pleadings), not a general contention or broad description of a claim. Furthermore, a request should further define the category of documents by providing a timeframe, which is tied to the relevant chronology of the case.[16]

help the tribunal by explaining in detail how and why the requested documents are relevant and material.
[15] For further reading, see: *The IBA Rules of the Taking of Evidence in International Arbitration: A Guide* by the author (Cambridge University Press, 2012).
[16] IBA Rules Article 3(3)(a)(ii) provides: 'A Request to Produce shall contain: ... (ii) a description in sufficient detail (including subject matter) of a narrow and specific requested

Failing to produce

[12–13 – 18] Guideline 14 obliges a Party Representative to explain to the Party whom he represents the necessity of producing, and potential consequences of failing to produce, any document that the Party or Parties have undertaken, or been ordered, to produce.[17] The tribunal will, of course, occasionally order a Party (rather than a Party Representative) to produce a specific document or documents. More often the tribunal will direct the production of a narrow and specific class of documents. This involves a search for responsive documents. This is the territory of Guideline 15 discussed below. Assuming that the Party has the document responsive to the Request it is another 'apple pie' truism that the Party needs to comply with the order or direction of the tribunal. Many Party Representatives will feel it unnecessary to volunteer advice to a sophisticated client that it needs to comply with the tribunal's direction; that will be self-evident from the fact that the tribunal made the direction.

[12–13 – 19] More problematic are the consequences of a failure to produce. Assuming the Party has made a search and unearthed responsive or potentially responsive documents that it is considering not producing, the competent (and honest) Party Representative would advise that the Party produces those documents that are responsive to the Request for that is consistent with the fundamental duties of complying with the tribunal's directions (i.e. complying with the arbitration agreement) and not misleading the tribunal (by omitting relevant (and presumably material) evidence). The consequences of a failure to produce might be many and various, including a loss of credibility, but the primary advice

category of Documents that are reasonably believed to exist; in the case of Documents maintained in electronic form, the requesting Party may, or the Arbitral Tribunal may order that it shall be required to, identify specific files, search terms, individuals or other means of searching for such Documents in an efficient and economical manner'. A production request must always be narrow and specific. For e-disclosure search parameters may assist in determining whether a request is narrow and specific.

[17] See generally *Myers* v. *Elman* [1940] AC 282 per Lord Atkin: 'What is the duty of the solicitor? . . . Obviously he must explain to his client what is the meaning of relevance; and equally obviously he must not necessarily be satisfied by the statement of his client that he has no documents, or no more than he chooses, to disclose. If he has reasonable grounds for supposing that there are others, he must investigate the matter.'

would have to be (a) to produce the documents; (b) that a refusal to produce is a breach of the tribunal's direction and hence a breach of the arbitration agreement; (c) that doing so amounts to offering false testimony (by omission) and hence counsel will or may have to withdraw; and (d) at the very least that the tribunal may draw an adverse inference from the failure to produce the documents which may be to a greater degree than the documents themselves might have given.

[12–13 – 20] The greater difficulty arises where the Party in its initial search finds a 'smoking gun' document. Clearly, it will not produce it as a document that is relied upon. The opposing Party in its Requests to Produce does not make a Request to which the document is responsive to although if he knew of the document it would clearly ask for it. Without more the document will not make it to the record. Here two competing obligations are in issue: the obligation of integrity and honesty under the Preamble to the Guidelines which might dictate that the document be adduced and the primary obligation to act in the Party's best interests under Guideline 3 which will dictate that provided there is no breach of the tribunal's directions that the document remain concealed. The answer is, it is suggested, clear. The primacy of the obligation under Guideline 3 prevails and there is nothing unethical in so doing.

[12–13 – 21] One matter that is to be welcomed from Guideline 14 is that it presupposes that the direction in relation a Request to Produce is aimed at the Party (rather than the Party Representative). Too often tribunals (and it is tempting to say 'lazy' tribunals) direct the Party Representative to undertake a search (or some variation of a search) and even to confirm that no responsive documents exist. Whilst it may be seen as a pragmatic and cost-effective response to a Request to Produce for the Party Representative to confirm that they have undertaken (or supervised) searches and that no responsive documents were unearthed – and the tribunal will invariably accept such an assurance – it does not prove or establish authority on the tribunal over the Party Representative. Purporting to exercise a jurisdiction that does not exist cannot create that very jurisdiction. Directions directed by the tribunal to a Party Representative may be politely declined.[18] Of course, this is subject to the agency argument advanced under Guidelines 1–3 above.

Advice on the search

[12–13 – 22] Guideline 15 addresses the Party Representative's obligation to advise that a proper search is undertaken and the responsive documents produced. If document production follows the IBA Rules this duty of search will arise only at the final stage[19] (although Party Representatives will usually advise that a full and comprehensive search is undertaken at an early stage so as to assess the case on the basis of all available evidence).

[12–13 – 23] The critics of Guideline 15 point to the double reasonableness test: "A Party Representative should advise . . . and assist . . . in taking, <u>reasonable</u> steps to ensure that . . . a <u>reasonable</u> search is made for Documents . . . " (emphasis added) as being doubly unintelligible. In truth, and in practice, the standard is not so complex that a Party Representative should have any difficulty in complying with the Guideline: giving advice of what needs to be done to achieve a stated result – the reasonable search. Knowing of the commonplace adoption of the IBA Rules or of practices consistent with them, a Party Representative who felt unable to give such advice and assistance (irrespective of the adoption of the Guidelines) should question whether he is competent to represent the Party.

[12–13 – 24] The initial production under the IBA Rules will be those documents that the Party wishes to rely upon.[20] Thereafter the opponent will usually make a Request to Produce and additional documents are often voluntarily produced in response to the Request. On each of these occasions the Party is producing

---

[18] What is often appropriate is to respond that, whilst not recognising any authority of the tribunal over the Party Representative, the Party Representative will, nevertheless, assist the Party to comply with the tribunal's order and will report accordingly to the tribunal.

[19] See the following paragraph.

[20] It could be argued that a party has undertaken through the IBA Rules (if adopted) to produce documents relied upon but this does not sit happily with Guideline 15(ii): that all non-privileged, responsive documents are produced unless responsive in this context means that they are responsive to the desire to rely upon them which would be a strange construction.

voluntarily and will not have undertaken to produce the documents nor will it have been directed to produce the documents.[21] Accordingly, even though some form of search will have been undertaken, Guideline 15 does not, strictly, apply. However, by using the words *'or that have been requested by another Party'* the Committee Comments indicates that the search obligation does apply to the stage of a Request to Produce. Although it may be good practice to undertake a proper search there is no obligation under Guideline 15 itself to do so unless, unusually, there is an undertaking or order to produce. At the stage of a Request to Produce there is usually no undertaking or order – at most, the Request to Produce may be built into a procedural timetable. There is no explanation for this tension. A proper search is a matter that the Party itself will see as good sense and efficient in the conduct of its own case, and hence these will probably be undertaken and probably at an early stage.

[12–13 – 25] The occasion that the second limb of Guideline 15, as opposed to the Committee Comments, really bites is when the tribunal considers the Request to Produce (usually, by then, in the form of a Redfern Schedule) and orders or directs a search be made in respect of such of the Requests as (a) have not been resolved by the parties themselves by agreement; (b) are pursued before the tribunal; and (c) the tribunal considers to be well-founded. On that occasion the Party Representative will, in practice, help the Party with its obligations under the order.

The required advice/assistance

[12–13 – 26] The degree of assistance that is required by the Party Representative is not defined. Some will consider it their duty to produce or ensure production of the responsive documents; others will consider it wholly a matter for the Party. As ever, some form of

---

21 Again it might be argued that a Party has undertaken through the IBA Rules (if adopted) to produce documents subject to a Request to Produce. Article 3(4) of the IBA Rules provides: 'Within the time ordered by the Arbitral Tribunal, the Party to whom the Request to Produce is addressed shall produce to the other Parties and, if the Arbitral Tribunal so orders, to it, all the Documents requested in its possession, custody or control as to which it makes no objection' (emphasis added). Again, the concluding words of the IBA Rules Article are difficult to read in a consistent manner with Guideline 15(ii).

mid-point/happy medium is the answer. The word "assist" implies, correctly, that the (primary) duty rests with the Party rather than the Party Representative. The assistance of the Party Representative may well not extend to a physical presence at collection sites – in larger cases this is often out-sourced to e-disclosure providers who harvest from computer systems. More probably, it will extend to initial advice on collection techniques such as focussing the search on key individuals, particular date ranges, the use of keyword searches in the case of electronic documents (ideally with agreed terms), whether a document or class is relevant, whether there is an obligation to produce duplicates and other issues of materiality, the treatment of backup media etc. Further advice will then usually be required as to whether particular documents are or are not responsive: often the product of the search is uploaded to computer-assisted review tools and reviewed by paralegals and others in the Party Representative's staff.

[12–13 – 27] An example of Party Representative assistance might be in advice as to whether it was unduly burdensome to produce documents (c.f. IBA Rules Article 9 (2) (c)). This often arises in the context of electronic documents. In the US Federal Rules of Civil Procedure, the (sensible) distinction is drawn between 'reasonably accessible' and 'not reasonably accessible' documents. The primary obligation is to produce from reasonably accessible documents. In US Federal litigation a party does not have to produce from documents that are not 'reasonably accessible because of undue burden or cost'.[22] The undue burden or cost can be 'trumped' by 'good cause' but then that can be subject to conditions, the most usual of which is that the requesting rather than the producing Party bears the cost of production.[23] It is another instance of balancing need and cost, and there can be no definitive answer that it will always be appropriate to act in one way or another.[24]

---

[22] Federal Rules of Civil Procedure 2007, Rule 26(b)(2)(B).

[23] Although doing so does not relieve the producing Party from considering the material for relevance and privilege, which may well be a considerable burden in itself.

[24] For examples of courts on both sides of the Atlantic grappling with these issues, see e.g. the US court case *Bullis* v. *Nichols*, 2005 WL 1838634 (W.D. Wash. Aug. 1, 2005) (in which the court refused to order the production of email on the basis that it would entail the production of 166,000 emails); and the English case, *Marlton* v. *Tectronix UK Holdings*

[12–13 – 28] The leading case in the area of accessibility in the US is *Zubulake* v. *UBS Warburg*.[25] *Zubulake* identified five categories of data accessibility and, hence, the burden of production.[26] The Sedona principles[27] likewise provide helpful guidelines to distinguish between accessible and inaccessible data. In assessing the balance between need and cost, the Advisory Committee Notes on the Federal Rules list seven helpful factors to bear in mind:

(1) The specificity of the discovery request;
(2) The quantity of information available from other more readily accessible sources;
(3) The failure to produce relevant information that seems likely to have existed but is no longer available either at all or from readily accessible sources;
(4) The likelihood of finding relevant material that cannot be obtained from other readily accessible sources;
(5) The perceived importance and usefulness of the information sought;

[2003] EWHC 383 (in which the court held that what might be reasonable in one case might not be in another).

[25] The various rounds of the litigation being reported at 217 F.R.D. 309 (S.D.N.Y. 2003), 229 F.R.D. 422 (S.D.N.Y. 2004), 220 F.R.D. 212 (S.D.N.Y. 2003) 216 F.R.D. 280 (S.D.N.Y. 2003).

[26] Those categories include: (1) active, online data accessed on a day-to-day basis; (2) 'near-line' data stored on optical or magnetic disks capable of being accessed automatically or by computerised means; (3) 'offline storage archives' such as those included in category (2) above but where manual intervention is required to access the data; (4) 'back-up tapes' which, because they mirror the computer structure, are unlikely to be organised for ease of searching, and; (5) 'erased, fragmented or damaged data' that can only be retrieved by significant processing. Generally, the first three categories of data are considered 'accessible' and the last two categories are considered 'inaccessible' (*W.E. Aubuchon Co. Inc.* v. *Benefirst LLC*, 245 F.R.D. 38 at 42 (D. Mass. 2007)).

[27] Available at https://thesedonaconference.org and an invaluable source of material on e-disclosure issues. See also the English Rules of Civil Procedure CPR 31B PD 21, which address the balancing exercise in assessing what is a reasonable search. The non-exhaustive list of matters that may be relevant as to the extent of a reasonable search is: (1) The number of documents involved. (2) The nature and complexity of the proceedings. (3) The ease and expense of retrieval of any particular document. This includes: (a) the accessibility of electronic documents; (b) the location of relevant electronic documents; (c) the likelihood of locating relevant data; (d) the cost of recovering any electronic documents; (e) the cost of disclosing and providing inspection of any relevant electronic documents; (f) the likelihood that electronic documents will be materially altered in the course of recovery, disclosure or inspection. (4) The availability of documents or contents of documents from other sources. (5) The significance of any document which is likely to be located during the search.

(6) The importance of the issues at stake in the litigation; and
(7) The parties' resources.

[12–13 – 29] At a practical level, the vast bulk of data that may require to be considered can be significantly reduced by running the population through a filter of 'keyword searches'[28] and de-duplication.[29] With the huge volumes of data now stored as email, it is often an unreasonably onerous task to manually review each document. In consequence, the discovery review is commonly limited by keyword searches. This filters out those documents <u>not</u> having one or more of the keywords present by allowing through the filter those that have one or more of the keywords. This can be an invaluable aid to a sensible, cost-effective and proportionate approach to disclosure and is expressly acknowledged by the IBA Rules in Article 3.3(a)(ii). However, running keyword searches over a large database can still be expensive and consequently it is advisable to agree on keyword lists as much as possible, or at least to be able to demonstrate that a fair and reasonable approach has been taken in performing the search. It is also important to consider, and if necessary to agree on, whether the search will extend to metadata and/or deleted items (or other categories of non-active data), since these sources of information can often be extremely revealing. *Digicel* v. *Cable & Wireless*[30] is an example of the court grappling with keyword searches.

[12–13 – 30] If there are serious issues but the burden and cost appear high, the arbitral tribunal may wish to consider a partial disclosure. An example of this is illustrated in *Zubulake* v. *UBS Warburg*,[31] a case involving an issue over the restoration of 77 backup tapes. The court ordered a sample of five tapes to be restored to assess the evidential value of the material and the cost of restoration. Similarly, in *Flexsys*

---

[28] Keyword searches are expressly recognised in the Practice Direction to the English Civil Procedure Rules Part 31 – Practice Direction 31B (paragraph 9(3)(b)): 'The parties and their legal representatives must also ... discuss the disclosure of Electronic Documents ... The discussions should include ... the tools and techniques ... to reduce the burden and cost of disclosure ... including ... the use of agreed Keyword Searches ...'. Keyword Searches are defined as meaning 'a software-aided search for words across the text of an Electronic Document'.
[29] Some studies show that effective filtering techniques by custodian, time and date, file size, keywords and de-duplication can reduce the number of documents to be reviewed by up to 75%.
[30] [2008] EWHC 2522 (Ch).   [31] 216 F.R.D. 280 (S.D.N.Y. 2003).

Americas LP v. *Kumho Tire USA Inc.*,[32] the court was faced with the issue of whether the plaintiff should produce documents relating to one custodian or from every employee. The court ordered production from ten custodians of the defendant's choice. In *Digicel* v. *Cable & Wireless*,[33] the court ordered the restoration of backup tapes sufficient to search the email accounts of seven individuals and, because of the difficulty of identifying the accounts, the parties were directed to 'meet and confer' and, thereafter, the lawyer for the party responsible for the restoration was to report progress every ten days or so to the other lawyer.

Proportionality

[12–13 – 31] Whether reasonable steps are taken and a reasonable search is undertaken are not the subject of guidance save that it is, according to the Committee guidance, also to be proportionate – but proportionate to what is not stated. Should it be to the overall amount in issue between the Parties or to the relevant importance of issues? The answer is probably a combination of both. If there is $1bn in dispute, that does not necessarily mean that every document going into even the smallest sub-issue should be assiduously searched for and produced: it may not be proportionate to do so. Similarly, if there is $100k in dispute, the key issue upon which liability turns might be worth an assiduous search and production. I suggest that the appropriate test is whether the anticipated outcome is proportionate to the potential impact that the document(s) might have with regard also to the sums involved, the importance of the issues, the complexity of the issues and the financial position of the parties.

[12–13 – 32] Very considerable sums can be spent on document production, and a handy cross-check is how the tribunal might view a subsequent claim for the costs of the search and production exercise. The tribunal might well ask for budgets for search and production costs if the proportionality of the forecast costs is in dispute.

---

[32] 1:05-CV-156, 2006 WL 3526794 (N.D. Ohio 6 December 2006).　　[33] *Supra*, n.18.

Concealment

[12–13 – 33] Guideline 16 appears to be another 'apple pie' truism. The process of document production under the IBA Rules, however, gives rise to potential problems. In the first instance of document production a Party will have to hand, it is assumed, most of the documents and will undertake a search for further relevant material. It will then sift those documents to assess those that are favourable and upon which it wishes to rely. Those will be produced under Article 3.1 of the IBA Rules. Those that are considered unhelpful will not be produced. Under the IBA Rules there cannot be suppression or concealment at this stage.

[12–13 – 34] The opponent will then make a Request to Produce. In doing so it will not know (it can speculate and infer, but will not usually know) what documents exist and are held by its opponent. It may be able to identify some specific documents[34] but will, more often, make a request for a class or category of documents.

[12–13 – 35] Upon receipt there will often be objection of a lack of specificity; a failure to identify, in the words of Article 3.3 of the IBA Rules, a narrow and specific category; or a lack of identified relevance and materiality. This type of objection may, and often will, find favour with the tribunal. The result is that the documents are not produced. There has been no undertaking or order to produce and yet material and material documents may thereby be suppressed and concealed. It does not, however, strictly amount to direct suppression or concealment of documents; rather, it is taking advantage of a legitimate objection, contemplated by the IBA Rules, that has the consequence of suppression or concealment.

[12–13 – 36] That may, however, breach the Preamble exhortations that Party Representatives should act with "integrity and honesty and should not engage in activities designed to produce unnecessary delay or expense, including tactics aimed at obstructing the arbitration proceedings".

---

[34] This will usually be those documents whose existence is self-evident from the documents that have been produced; i.e. they are mentioned or referred to in the documents that have been produced.

[12–13 – 37] If the tribunal then makes an order that some or all of the items on the Redfern Schedule be produced, clearly there may be already identified documents which are responsive and the non-production of which would clearly infringe Guideline 16 (and IBA Rules Article 3.4). There may, however, be legitimate issues over responsiveness that could create legitimate differences of opinion as to whether there is a breach.

Remedial action

[12–13 – 38] Guideline 17 is the remedial action arising from knowledge of a document that ought to have been produced not having been produced. Many of the same issues as are discussed above will arise.

Witnesses and experts

18. Before seeking any information from a potential Witness or Expert, a Party Representative should identify himself or herself, as well as the Party he or she represents, and the reason for which the information is sought.

19. A Party Representative should make any potential Witness aware that he or she has the right to inform or instruct his or her own counsel about the contact and to discontinue the communication with the Party Representative.

20. A Party Representative may assist Witnesses in the preparation of Witness Statements and Experts in the preparation of Expert Reports.

21. A Party Representative should seek to ensure that a Witness Statement reflects the Witness's own account of relevant facts, events and circumstances.

22. A Party Representative should seek to ensure that an Expert Report reflects the Expert's own analysis and opinion.

23. A Party Representative should not invite or encourage a Witness to give false evidence.

24. A Party Representative may, consistent with the principle that the evidence given should reflect the Witness's own account of relevant facts, events or circumstances, or the Expert's own analysis or opinion, meet or interact with Witnesses and Experts in order to discuss and prepare their prospective testimony.

25. A Party Representative may pay, offer to pay, or acquiesce in the payment of:
    (a) expenses reasonably incurred by a Witness or Expert in preparing to testify or testifying at a hearing;

(b) **reasonable compensation for the loss of time incurred by a Witness in testifying and preparing to testify; and**

(c) **reasonable fees for the professional services of a Party-appointed Expert.**

IBA COMMITTEE COMMENTS

Comments to Guidelines 18–25

Guidelines 18–25 are concerned with interactions between Party Representatives and Witnesses and Experts. The interaction between Party Representatives and Witnesses is also addressed in Guidelines 9–11 concerning Submissions to the Arbitral Tribunal.

Many international arbitration practitioners desire more transparent and predictable standards of conduct with respect to relations with Witnesses and Experts in order to promote the principle of equal treatment among Parties. Disparate practises among jurisdictions may create inequality and threaten the integrity of the arbitral proceedings.

The Guidelines are intended to reflect best international arbitration practise with respect to the preparation of Witness and Expert testimony.

When a Party Representative contacts a potential Witness, he or she should disclose his or her identity and the reason for the contact before seeking any information from the potential Witness (Guideline 18). A Party Representative should also make the potential Witness aware of his or her right to inform or instruct counsel about this contact and involve such counsel in any further communication (Guideline 19).

Domestic professional conduct norms in some jurisdictions require higher standards with respect to contacts with potential Witnesses who are known to be represented by counsel. For example, some common law jurisdictions maintain a prohibition against contact by counsel with any potential Witness whom counsel knows to be represented in respect of the particular arbitration.

If a Party Representative determines that he or she is subject to a higher standard than the standard prescribed in these Guidelines, he or she may address the situation with the other Party and/or the Arbitral Tribunal.

As provided by Guideline 20, a Party Representative may assist in the preparation of Witness Statements and Expert Reports, but should seek to ensure that a Witness Statement reflects the Witness's own account of relevant facts, events and circumstances (Guideline 21), and that any Expert Report reflects the Expert's own views, analysis and conclusions (Guideline 22).

A Party Representative should not invite or encourage a Witness to give false evidence (Guideline 23).

As part of the preparation of testimony for the arbitration, a Party Representative may meet with Witnesses and Experts (or potential Witnesses and Experts) to discuss their prospective testimony. A Party Representative may also help a Witness in preparing his or her own Witness Statement or Expert Report.

Further, a Party Representative may assist a Witness in preparing for their testimony in direct and cross-examination, including through practise questions and answers (Guideline 24). This preparation may include a review of the procedures through which testimony will be elicited and preparation of both direct testimony and cross-examination. Such contacts should however not alter the genuineness of the Witness or Expert evidence, which should always reflect the Witness's own account of relevant facts, events or circumstances, or the Expert's own analysis or opinion.

Finally, Party Representatives may pay, offer to pay or acquiesce in the payment of reasonable compensation to a Witness for his or her time and a reasonable fee for the professional services of an Expert (Guideline 25).

DISCUSSION

Transparency with witnesses

[18–25 – 1] Guideline 18 provides that a Party Representative should introduce himself; the Party he represents; and state the purpose of the enquiry when speaking to a potential witness or expert, and should do so at the outset of the conversation.

[18–25 – 2] As regards witnesses of fact, many of whom will be employed by the Party itself – and hence whose identity will be well known to the Party (and thus to the Party Representative who represents that Party) – the purpose of the enquiry may already be known. There will, however, be those who are not Party employees and it is important that they are not misled into thinking they are speaking to a different person or for a different purpose. The issue is most problematic with witnesses of fact who might make an unguarded comment. Expert witnesses are likely to be more circumspect; unlikely to have much to say of relevance without a greater degree of instruction, and any unguarded comment would be unlikely to be admissible before, or relevant to, the tribunal.

Upjohn/Miranda warnings

[18–25 – 3] Guideline 19 provides that the Party Representative should make a potential witness aware that he can instruct counsel of his choice and discontinue the contact.[1] Guideline 19 quite correctly does not, however, apply to expert witnesses. It is unusual for mere witnesses to engage counsel, although if they have been involved in, or are alleged to be involved in, wrongdoing, or wrongdoing that amounts to a serious criminal offence, it is understandable that they may wish to have independent counsel.

[18–25 – 4] The discontinuance of contact is plainly disjunctive rather than conjunctive to the instruction of counsel and the instruction of counsel is not a condition precedent to the right of the witness to discontinue contact.

The drafting of witness statements/expert reports

[18–25 – 5] Guideline 20 is one of the most fundamental Guidelines. It has to be read with Guideline 24: Guideline 20 concerns the preparation of a statement for the witness and Guideline 24 concerns the preparation of the witness to give evidence at an evidentiary hearing. Guideline 20 reflects IBA Rules Article 4.3, which provides:

---

[1] This is the arbitration equivalent of the 'Upjohn' warning (or corporate 'Miranda' warning – both are drawn from US proceedings) to potential witnesses: they involve telling a witness that the counsel is not the witness's counsel but counsel to the company and the witness has the right of silence. Of course, there might be cases where it might be appropriate to inform the witness that he might incriminate himself (and expose himself to potential criminal penalties) and might therefore wish not to answer questions. In those rare cases, some form of warning might be advisable.

'It shall not be improper for a Party, its officers, employees, legal advisors or other representatives to interview its witnesses or potential witnesses and to discuss their prospective testimony with them.' The Guideline, however, goes further and permits the Party Representative to "assist" the witness to prepare a statement, or an expert a report. Neither quite reflects the common way that factual statements are now produced: that the witness will be interviewed by the lawyer or counsel who will, on the basis of that interview, draft a statement for the witness. The IBA Rule word 'discussion' and the Guideline word "assistance" are both rather coy over the reality that the Party Representative will interview a witness and draft a statement on that basis.

[18–25 – 6] Nevertheless, this is welcome clarification due to the widely different approaches across common law and civil law professions. In some civil law jurisdictions it would be a breach of ethical and professional rules to even speak to a witness, but, for example, in the US, it would be negligent not to do so.[2] The advantage of Party Representatives assisting in the preparation of statements is that they ought to respond to the issues, be logically structured, and ensure that basic grammatical structures are followed.

Assisting witnesses

[18–25 – 7] To 'discuss' or "assist" are broad concepts. It has to be assumed that they are intended to be consistent (although why the same words were not used is a mystery), and would probably encompass preparing a witness statement in the manner outlined above (certainly permissible under, for example, English rules), but not

---

[2] The Comments and Illustrations section of Restatement (Third) of the Law, Law Governing Lawyers s.116, provides: 'Preparing a witness may include: discussing the witness's recollection and probable testimony; revealing to the witness other testimony and evidence that will be presented and asking the witness to reconsider the witness's recollection or recounting of events in that light; discussing the applicability of law to the events in issue; reviewing the factual context into which the witness's observations and opinions will fit; reviewing document or other physical evidence that may be introduced; and discussing the probable lines of hostile cross-examination that the witness should be prepared to meet. Witness preparation may include rehearsal of testimony. A lawyer may suggest [to the witness] choice of words that might be employed to make the witness's meaning clear.'

'coaching', which is not permissible, and is certainly not permissible if the "assistance" goes so far as to suggest the testimony that the witness might give in a statement, beyond clarifying or giving clarity by a choice of words. Clearly there is a world of difference between a witness expressing himself inelegantly and, in consequence, counsel suggesting a concise form of alternative words that the witness confirms is his evidence, on the one hand, and, on the other, counsel taking the initiative and suggesting to the witness what his evidence might be on a particular topic. The former, I suggest, is perfectly proper; the latter is not.

[18–25 – 8] Ultimately, each lawyer will be governed by his own ethical and professional rules as to what can and cannot be done, although double deontology means that this may not be an easy answer. The different standards applicable to individual Party Representatives will not create a completely level playing field where counsel are in different jurisdictions, but the Guideline will assist in levelling the playing field. The simple fact of the issue being raised (whether by the Parties, the Party Representatives or the tribunal) may enable greater clarification on what is, and is not, permitted from the tribunal at an early stage – typically the IBA Rules Article 2 consultation (the first procedural meeting).

[18–25 – 9] The Guideline is, as ever, a compromise between different practices, with perhaps US practice and some civil jurisdictions being polar opposites. The former has the practice of heavily influencing the content of witness evidence – coaching witnesses (i.e. preparing them for lines of cross-examination) and conducting a mock evidentiary hearing in advance of the actual hearing – whereas the latter may prevent all contact. Indeed, witness contact might well amount to criminal offences if undertaken by counsel from a civil law background and would certainly amount to serious professional misconduct. Even among the common law jurisdictions there is a wide disparity. English counsel, for example, are not permitted to coach witnesses, whereas US counsel are (although see below for further discussion on this). Some international law firms ruthlessly expose these differences by, for example, simply having their US counsel do what their English colleagues, for example, are prevented from doing.

[18–25 – 10] These seemingly stark differences between US practice and the practice in other jurisdictions might, however, not be as far apart as they might seem. Certainly, in court proceedings in the UK, evidence in chief (or direct evidence) is given by the witness making a written statement in advance of oral testimony and the oral evidence does little more than to confirm the truth of that statement. This practice is very often followed in international arbitration: for example, the IBA Rules in Article 4.4 provides for witness statements from witnesses of fact, and Article 4.3 sanctions counsel interviewing witnesses and discussing testimony. The Guidance to the Rules provides that witness statements "...may be considered as the 'evidence in chief' ('direct evidence') so that extensive explanation by the witness becomes superfluous and examination by the other party can start almost immediately."

[18–25 – 11] The written statements relied upon by UK courts or in arbitral references are often very carefully crafted by counsel and, although they ought to reflect the words of the witness, they are often the words that counsel would like them to use. As discussed above, counsel may suggest a form of words that more felicitously expresses the witness's testimony. For example, for some reason of modern culture, it is common in England, and perhaps elsewhere, for the word 'went' to be used for speech; e.g. 'He went "yeah".' This could be suggested to be 'He said "yes".' But, this uncontroversial behaviour does not disguise the degree of preparation that goes into a witness statement. Before those from outside the US get too exercised by the US 'coaching', they should have a good look at their own involvement in the drafting of witness statements.[3]

Witness's own words

[18–25 – 12] The safeguard to Guideline 20 is Guidelines 21, 22 and 24. The latter Guidelines provide that the witness statement must reflect the witness's own account of the relevant events: in effect, it is

---

[3] Written witness testimony, compared to oral evidence in chief, provides a far greater opportunity for counsel to shape, direct and influence the evidence. Demeanour and credibility are more easily assessed with oral evidence in chief but that benefit is usually sacrificed in the quest for efficiency.

his own words. It is a fairly modest objective. The Party Representative must do no more than 'seek [i.e. try] to ensure' that it reflects the witness's 'own account'. The word 'own' is presumably there to emphasise that it is to be the witness's words rather than, presumably, the Party Representative's; but, it is suggested, this does not prevent counsel from suggesting more concise, elegant or simply better wording, provided that the witness is content with that wording and confirms that it is his evidence.

[18–25 – 13] Guideline 22 is the equivalent of Guideline 21, but for experts rather than witnesses of fact. It is unlikely that issues will arise with professional expert witnesses, whose reputation is normally worth more than might be gained by being less than honest and frank. The independence and reputation of the expert is a self-regulating check on the contents of the expert's report. German arbitration law permits a Party to challenge a tribunal-appointed expert on the grounds of justifiable doubts as to independence or impartiality on the same basis that an arbitrator could be challenged. Any challenge is likely to arise either when a report is served or when the expert is called to give evidence. However, it is clear, at least in England, that the fact of a close personal friendship or professional acquaintance does not, of itself, prohibit an expert from giving evidence.[4] Clearly, however, it may contribute to the weight that a tribunal puts on that evidence. Equally, again at least in England, an employee of a party can, in theory, give expert evidence; but again, the weight attributed to the evidence may then be (considerably) less.[5]

Expert's duties

[18–25 – 14] The expert must clearly assist the tribunal to the best of his ability and tell the truth. In the English case of *The Ikarian*

---

[4] *Liverpool Roman Catholic Archdiocesan Trustees* v. *Goldberg Times*, 9 March 2001. The subsequent decision of the trial judge to exclude the evidence reported at [2001] 1 WLR 2337 was disapproved by the Court of Appeal in *R (Factortame Limited)* v. *Transport Secretary (No. 8)* [2003] QB 381.
[5] *Field* v. *Leeds City Council* (2000) 32 HLR 619.

Reefer,[6] Cresswell J set out the duties of an expert to the court.[7] Although not binding in international commercial arbitration, the guidelines are of good general application and have been widely accepted in many jurisdictions:

> *I will refer to some of the duties and responsibilities of experts in civil cases because I consider that a misunderstanding on the part of certain expert witnesses ... as to their duties and responsibilities contributed to the length of the trial ...*

1. *Expert evidence presented to the [tribunal] should be and should be seen to be the independent product of the expert uninfluenced as to form or content by the exigencies of litigation ...*
2. *An expert witness should provide independent assistance to the [tribunal] by way of objective unbiased opinion in relation to matters within his expertise ... An expert witness ... should never assume the role of advocate.*
3. *An expert witness should state the facts or assumptions on which his opinion is based. He should not omit to consider material facts which detract from his concluded opinion ...*
4. *An expert witness should make it clear when a particular question or issue falls outside his expertise.*
5. *If an expert's opinion is not properly researched because he considers that insufficient data is available then this must be stated with an indication that the opinion is no more than a provisional one ...*
6. *If, after exchange of reports, an expert witness changes his view on a material matter ... such change of view should be communicated ... to the other side without delay and when appropriate to the [tribunal].*
7. *Where expert evidence refers to photographs, plans, calculations ... survey reports or other similar documents there must be provided to the opposite party at the same time as the exchange of reports ...* [8]

---

[6] *National Justice Compania Naviera SA* v. *Prudential Assurance Co. Ltd* [1993] 2 Lloyd's Rep 68, at 81.

[7] The judgment was overturned on appeal, but nothing casts any doubt on these guidelines, which are generally accepted to be of universal application.

[8] In practice, all – or the vast majority – of these should have been produced at the stage of document production.

Review of draft expert reports

[18–25 – 15] Even within the confines of these Guidelines it is never-theless routine for experts to provide draft reports for comment by counsel. In *Moore* v. *Getahun*[9] (a decision of the Ontario Court of Appeal overturning the notorious first instance decision) the Court held that the judge had erred in holding that it was unacceptable for counsel to review and discuss a draft expert report. In doing so the Court of Appeal held:

- banning undocumented discussions between counsel and expert or mandating disclosure of all written communications is unsup-ported by, and contrary to, existing authority;
- counsel's review of a draft report is important and enables counsel to ensure that the report complies with the relevant court rules and the rules of evidence, addresses only relevant issues before the Court, is accessible and comprehensible to its audience, and is responsive to pertinent legal issues;
- draft reports and communications between counsel and expert are privileged and need not be disclosed;
- consultation between counsel and expert is essential so as to ensure that the expert knows his duties and responsibilities;
- there are existing mechanisms designed to ensure the objectivity and independence of the expert, including counsel's ethical duties preventing counsel from interfering with the independence and objectivity of the expert; the expert's own ethical duties; and the expert being subject to being cross-examined on his report.

[18–25 – 14] These guidelines are helpful and could, and should, be readily adapted to arbitration. They should stand alongside the *The Ikarian Reefer* guidance.

Preparation of witnesses for testimony

[18–25 – 15] Guideline 24 deals with the phase after the service of witness statements and before oral testimony at an evidential hearing. The Guideline permits the Party Representative to "meet or interact"

[9] 2015 ONCA 55.

with witnesses and experts in order to "discuss and prepare" their prospective testimony. The safeguard is that all interaction must be consistent with the overriding aim of ensuring the evidence is in the words of the witness.

[18–25 – 16] Only the strictest regimes might seek to prevent a meeting of some sort between counsel and witnesses, and it is a small step to "interact" with them. The degree of interaction is, however, more problematic. At one level, such things as to tell the witness of the layout of the room where the evidential hearing will take place, whether they can be present when other witnesses give evidence, the order in which things will be done and how to address the tribunal, are matters that are likely to be uncontroversial. More difficult will be US-style coaching and mock cross-examination (discussed below) followed by training tips on how to improve, including suggested 'better' answers.

[18–25 – 17] The answer, as ever, is somewhere in between and derives from a proper understanding of the proper purpose of the interaction as set out in the Guidelines: to "discuss and prepare" their testimony. The Guidance states that: "This preparation may include a review of the procedures through which testimony will be elicited and preparation of both direct testimony and cross-examination." The "review of the procedures" is unlikely to be controversial and presumably will focus at the lower end of the "interaction" discussed above: such things as the layout of the room etc. Much more difficult is the "preparation of … testimony". Assuming the acceptance of any form of "preparation", the question that must arise is the extent of the "preparation".

Acceptable preparation

[18–25 – 18] What is likely to be acceptable "preparation" is reminding a witness (a) to re-read the pleadings and his statement; (b) to read identified passages from other witness statements (those perceived to be relevant); (c) the key documents on the record on the topics that the witness gives evidence upon; and, possibly, (d) the key factual issues in the reference (there are issues with the legal context – see below).

[18–25 – 19] As "direct testimony" is likely to be perfunctory, there is likely to be less scope for artful preparation of direct testimony: witnesses of fact are usually sworn, confirm the truth of their statement, answer a (very) few clarification questions or questions arising from statements they have not had a chance to answer (e.g. rebuttal statements), and are then tendered for cross-examination.

[18–25 – 21] The preparation is, accordingly, most importantly of cross-examination and it is material to note that the preparation is "of" rather than 'for' cross-examination: like all other words in the Guidelines, these were no doubt agonised over by the drafting committee. 'For' would have been far less controversial, and it must be assumed that the choice of words is deliberate and conscious. In England, for example, where coaching is prohibited, there are commercial organisations that train or 'familiarise' witnesses using an entirely different set of hypothetical facts that the witness will learn and then play the role of giving evidence. Using the actual facts of a particular case is prohibited. That degree of preparation – by using hypothetical facts – might be consistent with preparation 'for' cross-examination. It is difficult to construe the wording of the Guidelines as anything other than something that condones witness preparation in the sense of coaching and mock cross-examination on the actual facts: it is preparation "of" the cross-examination, and the wording must have the meaning as if the words *'that they will be subject to'* were inserted at the end of the Committee Comments.

US Witness preparation

[18–25 – 22] The word "of" can only derive from US practice. The US practice is known as 'horse-shedding' or 'wood-shedding' the witness – so-named after the practice of attorneys who lingered in sheds near the old courthouse in White Plains, New York to rehearse their witnesses.

[18–25 – 23] Notwithstanding the near universal practice in the US there is, however, no rule in the US that clearly states what is and is not permissible. The American Bar Association Model Rules of Professional Conduct provide ethical guidance: a lawyer must not knowingly 'offer evidence that the lawyer knows to be false'[10] or 'counsel or assist a witness to testify falsely'.[11] So far, so good.

[18–25 – 24] A lawyer must balance these obligations against the obligation to competently represent the client: "Competent representation requires the legal knowledge, skill, thoroughness and preparation reasonably necessary for the representation".[12] The tension arises from the Committee Comments: '*Fair competition in the adversary system is secured by prohibitions against destruction or concealment of evidence, improperly coaching witnesses, obstructive tactics in discovery procedure and the like*'[13] (emphasis added). The plain inference is that by outlawing 'improperly' coaching witnesses there is an endorsement of 'properly' coaching witnesses.

[18–25 – 25] Section 116 of the Restatement (Third) of the Law Governing Lawyers (2000) provides:

In preparing a witness to testify, a lawyer may invite the witness to provide truthful testimony favourable to the lawyer's client. Preparation consistent with the Rule of this section may include the following:
Discussing the role of the witness and effective courtroom demeanor;
Discussing the witness's recollection and probable testimony;
Revealing to the witness other testimony or evidence that will be presented and asking the witness to reconsider the witness's recollection or recounting of events in that light;
Discussing the applicability of law to the events in issue
Reviewing the factual context into which the witness's observations or opinions will fit;
Reviewing documents or other physical evidence that may be introduced; and
Discussing probable lines of cross-examination that the witness should be prepared to meet.
Witness preparation may include the rehearsal of testimony. A lawyer may suggest [a] choice of words that might be employed to make the witness's meaning clear. However, a lawyer may not assist the witness to testify falsely as to a matter of fact.

[18–25 – 26] The essence of this obligation is summed up in a marvellously expressive phrase explaining the lawyer's duty as being to "extract the facts from the witness, not to pour them into him; to

---

[10] Rule 3.3(a)(3).
[11] Rule 3.4 and see Restatement (Third) of the Law Governing Lawyers §120(1) (2000).
[12] Rule 1.1.   [13] Comment to Rule 3.4.

learn what the witness does know, not to teach him what he does not know."[14] Witness preparation should be, at most, 'how' to testify, not 'what' to testify about.

English witness preparation

[18–25 – 27] In England, the Bar's Code of Conduct is clear: 'A barrister must not … rehearse, practice or coach a witness in relation to his evidence.'[15] The Solicitors' Code of Conduct is less clear in stating that witness coaching may amount to an attempt to influence a witness and so mislead the court but it is not clearly prohibited.[16] The standard is widely accepted to be set by a statement that:

> The witness should give his or her own evidence, so far as practicable unin-
> fluenced by what anyone else has said, whether in formal discussions or informal
> conversations. The rule, indeed hopefully avoids any possibility, that one witness
> may tailor his evidence in light of what anyone else said, and equally, avoids any
> unfounded perception that he may have done so. These risks are inherent in
> witness training. Even if the training takes place one-to-one with someone
> completely remote from the facts of the case itself, the witness may come, even
> unconsciously, to appreciate which aspects of his evidence are perhaps not quite
> consistent with what others are saying, or indeed not quite what is required of
> him. An honest witness may alter the emphasis of his evidence to accommodate
> what he thinks may be a different, more accurate, or simply better remembered
> perception of events.[17]

[18–25 – 28] Approval was given to 'pre-trial arrangements to famil-
iarize the witness with the layout of the court, the likely sequence of

[14] *In re Eldridge* 82 NY 161, 171 (1880). See also *Geders* v. *United States* 425 US 80, 90 n3 (1976): 'An attorney must respect the important ethical distinction between discussing testimony and seeking improperly to influence it.'
[15] Paragraph 705. Note also the Bar Standards Board: Guidance on Witness Preparation (October, 2005): It should be 'borne in mind … that there is a distinction, when interview-ing a witness, between questioning him closely in order to enable him to present his evidence fully and accurately or in order to test the reliability of his evidence (which is permissible) and questioning him with a view to encouraging the witness to alter, massage, or obscure his real recollection (which is not).'
[16] Virtually the same rule applies to solicitor advocates: The Law Society's Code of Conduct for Advocacy §6.5(b). The fact that a different standard applies to solicitor advocates and solicitors who are not advocating may be significant.
[17] *R* v. *Momodou* [2005] EWCA Crim 177 at [61] – although a criminal case it is widely accepted to be equally applicable to civil matters: see *Ultraframe* v. *Fielding* [2005] EWHC 1638.

events when the witness is giving evidence, and a balanced appraisal of the different responsibilities of the different participants ... none of this however involves discussions about proposed or intended evidence'.[18]

[18–25 – 29] In light of this, the English practice is to permit witness familiarisation: this includes permitting familiarising the witness with court or arbitral procedures; informing the witness of the need to testify clearly by listening to and answering the question, by speaking slowly and by avoiding irrelevant comments; and tips as to how to survive the rigours of cross-examination. As the leading provider puts it: 'Mock questioning is expressly permitted to give a witness greater familiarity and confidence in the process of giving oral evidence, provided the exercise is not based on facts which are the same as or similar to those of any current or impending trial.' And as the Bar Council puts it: '[M]ock cross-examination or rehearsals of particular lines of questioning that counsel proposes to follow are not permitted ... great care must be taken not to do or say anything which could be interpreted as suggesting that the witness should say, or how he or she should express himself or herself in the witness box – that would be coaching.'[19]

Witness preparation in other jurisdictions

[18–25 – 30] Other countries where codes of conduct prohibit witness preparation by attorneys include Belgium, Italy, France[20] and Switzerland. The issue has also been brought before the Trial Chamber of the International Criminal Court at The Hague. Analysing the practice in a number of countries, including Australia, Canada, the US and England, the court said:

[T]he preparation of witness testimony by parties prior to trial may diminish what would otherwise be helpful spontaneity during the giving of evidence by a witness. The spontaneous nature of testimony can be of paramount importance

---

[18] *Id.* at [62].
[19] Bar Council Guidance on Preparation of Witness Statements – Preparing Witness Statements for use in Civil Proceedings – Dealings with Witnesses §12[2] October 2005.
[20] Note, however, the Paris Bar Council Resolution of 26 February 2008: 'In the context of international arbitration seated in France or elsewhere, it is permissible for counsel to prepare a witness before his or her oral examination.' See Paris Bar Bulletin, 2008 no. 9, p. 4.

to the Court's ability to find the truth, and the Trial Chamber is not willing to lose such an important element in the proceedings.[21]

[18–25 – 31] The Trial Chamber acknowledged the distinction between witness 'proofing' and witness 'familiarisation'. The Chamber defined the former as the 'practice whereby a meeting is held between a party to the proceedings and witness before the witness is due to testify in Court, the purpose of which is to re-examine the witness's evidence to enable more accurate, complete and efficient testimony'. The latter was defined as 'assisting the witnesses to understand fully the Court proceedings and the roles that they and the participants play in them. The practice would also involve explaining the process of direct examination and cross-examination.'

[18–25 – 32] The Trial Chamber explained its decision as follows:

While witness familiarisation as defined in this decision will be permitted as well as the practice of providing a witness for the sole purpose of refreshing memory, with his or her previous statements prior to testimony in Court, the practice of 'witness proofing' … is prohibited.

Particular issues

[18–25 – 33] One particular problem is group preparation with more than one witness being prepared at a time. Expressly or by implication, there may be a message that testimony should be consistent among the group and individuals may be persuaded that they recall what others recall.

[18–25 – 34] Many of the larger US law firms have mock courtrooms to enable practice testimony sessions to take place in as real conditions as possible. This openly extends to mock trials before mock jurors to see how witnesses are evaluated in a court environment, and this practice extends also to mock tribunals. The aim of these sessions is to work out what needs to be fixed before the real trial/evidentiary

---

[21] Decision Regarding the Practices Used to Prepare and Familiarise Witnesses for Giving Testimony at Trial No. ICC-01/04-01/06 30 November 2007.

hearing. The steps can include a digital running assessment of the performance of witnesses (and counsel) that can be presented graphically.

[18–25 – 35] The proponents of these practices contend that they merely teach witnesses techniques for answering questions. They seek to make it clear why volunteering information to opposing counsel is not helpful; they seek to help witnesses understand the theme of their testimony and its relationship to the case.

[18–25 – 36] They also address less controversial areas such as the difference between direct and cross-examination; how to address the tribunal; distracting mannerisms; inappropriate attitudes; volume and speed; how to deal with a mistake; and how to ask for a break and similar matters.

Witnesses and legal context

[18–25 – 37] Another particular issue is telling the witness of the legal context in which their testimony is relevant (endorsed by the Restatement (Third) of the Law Governing Lawyers). One school of thought is that it helps the witness understand the context of their evidence, whereas others fear it might influence the testimony. For the latter, regard only needs to be paid to the book and film, *Anatomy of a Murder*, in which the lawyer is defending a man charged with the murder of his wife's rapist. The lawyer runs through the available legal defences to murder and pauses to suggest the client consider his position. The client then contends that he had temporary insanity (one of the recognised defences the lawyer has just advised exists). It is not difficult to contemplate a lawyer perfectly properly advising a client on the legal issues in a case where the principal witness is the client himself and the client emphasising in his testimony the necessary ingredients of the cause of action or defence.

Experts

[18–25 – 38] Guideline 24 also addresses expert reports. The comments above relating to experts in Guideline 20 apply equally here.

Payments to witnesses

[18–25 – 39] Guideline 25 provides for the payment of expenses to witnesses of fact and experts, the payment of compensation for time given to witnesses of fact and a fee to experts. This reflects the practice that a Party is, of course, perfectly at liberty to meet the expenses of a witness in attending an evidentiary hearing. This will normally include travel and accommodation costs. A Party can also properly compensate a witness for time devoted to the reference either at a normal hourly or daily rate. Provided there is no element of bounty in this, it is perfectly acceptable under most laws. Clearly, an expert will be entitled to a fee and it is less likely that any reputable expert will fall foul of this Guideline or put the Party Representative in any difficulty.

[18–25 – 40] As the American Bar Association Model Rules of Professional Conduct puts it, a lawyer should not 'counsel or assist a witness to testify falsely, or offer an inducement to a witness that is prohibited by law'.[22] The accompanying Guidance provides that:

[I]t is not improper to pay a witness's expenses ... on terms permitted by law. The common law rule in most jurisdictions is that it is improper to pay an occurrence[23] witness any fee for testifying ...

[18–25 – 41] The Guidance might appear, at first reading, to outlaw any payment of a fee as opposed to expenses, but this is not the case. The American Bar Association Standing Committee on Ethics and Professional Responsibility has issued a formal opinion[24] which states: '... compensating a witness for loss of time which he could have devoted to other pursuits does not constitute payment of an "expense" incurred by the witness. Nor, on the other hand, does compensating a witness for his loss of time amount to paying him a "fee for testifying".' The Committee noted that the Model Rules of Professional Conduct replaced a Model Code which expressly provided that 'a lawyer may ... acquiesce in the payment of ... reasonable compensation to a witness for his loss of time in attending and testifying ...' and continued that 'there is nothing in the history

---

[22] Rule 3.4(b).
[23] An 'occurrence' witness is simply another manner of describing a witness of fact.
[24] ABA Formal Opinion 96–402.

of Rule 3.4(b) to indicate that the drafters of the model Rules intended to negate this concept …'. The Committee further noted that certain statutes expressly permitted the payment of lay witnesses for 'the reasonable value of time lost in attendance at any such trial, hearing or proceeding'.[25]

[18–25 – 42] This ability to compensate a witness extends to a reasonable amount of time spent preparing to testify, including time spent in reviewing and researching material. As a matter of good practice, it should always be made clear that the fee is not for the substance or efficacy of the evidence but to compensate for lost time.

[18–25 – 43] There will, however, always be limits on what is proper. In *Golden Door Jewelry Creations* v. *Lloyds Underwriters Non-Marine Association*,[26] the court held the insurer's attorneys had violated Rule 3.4(b) by acquiescing in the payment of two witnesses of fact. For the original information, one was paid US$100,000, the other US$25,000; for depositions, one was paid US$95,000, the other US$25,000; for living expenses, one was paid US$65,000, the other US$22,000; and for appearing as a witness at a criminal trial, one was paid US$72,000.

[18–25 – 44] In terms of assessing what is reasonable, the New York State Bar Association Committee on Professional Ethics has said:

We must attempt to draw the line between compensation that enhances the truth seeking process by easing the burden of testifying witnesses, and compensation that serves to hinder the truth seeking process because it tends to 'influence' witnesses to 'remember' things in a way favourable to the side paying him.

[18–25 – 45] The California State Bar has contributed that: 'Possible objective bases upon which to determine reasonable compensation might include the witness' rate of pay if currently employed, what the witness last earned if currently unemployed, or what others might earn for comparable activity'[27] and the State Bar of Arizona has pithily summed matters up: 'a fee may appear unreasonable if the fee is so high that the witness is "better off" than she would have

---

[25] 18 U.S.C. §201(j).   [26] 865 F. Supp. 1516 (1994).
[27] California State Bar Standing Committee on Professional Responsibility and Conduct, Formal Opinion 1997–149.

been if she spent the time otherwise earning an income rather than testifying or preparing to testify'.[28]

[18–25 – 46] In England, the Solicitors Code of Conduct paragraph 11.07 provides:

You must not make, or offer to make, payments to a witness dependent upon the nature of the evidence given or upon the outcome of the case.

[18–25 – 47] The Guidance to the rule provides that "There is no objection to your paying reasonable expenses to witnesses and reasonable compensation for loss of time attending court."

[18–25 – 48] All of this Guidance appears pragmatic and will no doubt assist tribunals faced with a challenge to a witness (or the evidence of that witness) who is being paid. Plainly, problems arise where either the evidence is paid for, whether by paying a fee, paying expenses that are unrelated to and exceed actual cost, or by paying on the result of the evidence or the claim. Anything in excess of strict reimbursement of expenses and proper compensation for time is wrongful, and not only would the amounts so paid be irrecoverable as costs if that party were successful and entitled to costs, but the weight to be attached to the witness's evidence would be seriously affected by the fact of such payment, and the tribunal could properly reject the evidence in its entirety if it felt that the payment so undermined the evidence as to make it of no credibility. If counsel were conscious of the payment, there could also be professional sanctions for him.

---

[28] State Bar of Arizona Committee on the Rules of Professional Conduct, Formal Opinion 1997–07.

Remedies for Misconduct

26. If the Arbitral Tribunal, after giving the Parties notice and a reasonable opportunity to be heard, finds that a Party Representative has committed Misconduct, the Arbitral Tribunal, as appropriate, may:
    (a) admonish the Party Representative;
    (b) draw appropriate inferences in assessing the evidence relied upon, or the legal arguments advanced by, the Party Representative;
    (c) consider the Party Representative's Misconduct in apportioning the costs of the arbitration, indicating, if appropriate, how and in what amount the Party Representative's Misconduct leads the Tribunal to a different apportionment of costs;
    (d) take any other appropriate measure in order to preserve the fairness and integrity of the proceedings.
27. In addressing issues of Misconduct, the Arbitral Tribunal should take into account:
    (a) the need to preserve the integrity and fairness of the arbitral proceedings and the enforceability of the award;
    (b) the potential impact of a ruling regarding Misconduct on the rights of the Parties;
    (c) the nature and gravity of the Misconduct, including the extent to which the Misconduct affects the conduct of the proceedings;
    (d) the good faith of the Party Representative;
    (e) relevant considerations of privilege and confidentiality; and

(f) **the extent to which the Party represented by the Party Representative knew of, condoned, directed, or participated in, the Misconduct.**

IBA COMMITTEE COMMENTS

Comments to Guidelines 26–27

Guidelines 26–27 articulate potential remedies to address Misconduct by a Party Representative.

Their purpose is to preserve or restore the fairness and integrity of the arbitration.

The Arbitral Tribunal should seek to apply the most proportionate remedy or combination of remedies in light of the nature and gravity of the Misconduct, the good faith of the Party Representative and the Party whom he or she represents, the impact of the remedy on the Parties' rights, and the need to preserve the integrity, effectiveness and fairness of the arbitration and the enforceability of the award.

Guideline 27 sets forth a list of factors that is neither exhaustive nor binding, but instead reflects an overarching balancing exercise to be conducted in addressing matters of Misconduct by a Party Representative in order to ensure that the arbitration proceed in a fair and appropriate manner.

Before imposing any remedy in respect of alleged Misconduct, it is important that the Arbitral Tribunal gives the Parties and the impugned Representative the right to be heard in relation to the allegations made.

DISCUSSION

Consequences of Misconduct

[26–27 – 1] Guidelines 26 and 27 provide the remedies for Misconduct[1] and can be seen as both the heart and the logical conclusion of the Guidelines. If there are Guidelines without sanction it might be questioned whether the Guidelines were nothing

---

[1] Note the definition of Misconduct and the discussion under the Definitions section above.

but toothless aspirations. There are those who question whether the potential for sanctions, and the mere fact of the existence of the potential remedy, acts as a real deterrent for those intent on guerrilla tactics: if a Party Representative is going to behave in a reprehensible manner and contrary to other of the Guidelines, will he really be deterred by the prospect of an admonishment from an *ad hoc* tribunal?

Powers – not obligations

[26–27 – 2] It is worth stressing that the powers of the tribunal are just that: powers – there is no obligation on the tribunal to either make a finding of any alleged breach or, in the event of such a finding, to impose a sanction. This is evident from the opening word "if" and the word "may" before the list of potential sanctions. This is the same approach as exists under the LCIA Rules; it enables a tribunal to exercise such power consistent with its obligation to conduct the reference in a fair, efficient and expeditious manner. Tribunals would be well advised, absent consent to the adoption of the Guidelines, to consider whether sanctions are necessary to safeguard the integrity and fairness of the proceedings. Only if there is no other option should the tribunal proceed to consider direct sanctions against the Party Representative.

Jurisdiction

[26–27 – 3] The first question must be to establish (or at least decide) whether the tribunal has the power to sanction counsel, and, if so, where that power derives from.[2] One thing that is clear is that the

---

[2] Note that in the US, tribunals appear to have no power to disqualify counsel: *Munich Reinsurance America Inc.* v. *ACE Prop & Cas Ins Co* 500 F.Supp.2d 272 (2007): 'Disqualification of an attorney for an alleged conflict of interest is a substantive matter for the Court and not arbitrators. Attorney discipline has historically been a matter for judges and nor arbitrators because it requires an application of substantive state law regarding the legal profession.' And see: *Northwestern Nat'l Insurance Co.* v. *INSCO Ltd.* No. 11 Civ. 1124(SAS), 2011 WL 4552997 at 5 (SDNY 3 October 2011) '[a]ttorney disqualification is a "substantive matter for the courts and not arbitrators" for the simple reason that "it requires an application of substantive state law regarding the legal profession". In other words, arbitrators are selected by the parties to a dispute primarily for their "expertise in the particular industries engaged in" and cannot be expected to be familiar with the standards

standards of behaviour and ethics – whether of a national bar (or
similar) or international standards (whether the Guidelines or otherwise) – are irrelevant to the existence of the power. Those standards
are enforceable by professional bodies or national courts and not the
tribunal or the administering institution. Absent express power, the
proponents argue that the power is a function of the consent to
arbitrate, Party autonomy and the Parties' agreement to arbitrate
rather than via recourse to state courts. The traditional argument is
that, by consenting to arbitrate, the Parties bestow on the tribunal a
power to decide how the reference is to be conducted. A function of
having the power to determine how the reference is to be conducted
is to control counsel that appear before the tribunal. The alternative
is the agency basis (which can be seen as a simple development of
the traditional theory) discussed above in the Discussion under
Guidelines 1–3. The argument that the tribunal has no jurisdiction
and, rather, that state courts have exclusive jurisdiction is not entirely
persuasive. The tribunal may have to decide many things for which
they might have no particular expertise, e.g. foreign law, and it is
invariably more convenient to have everything decided in the reference rather than a multitude of different proceedings. Of course, that
means neither (a) that the tribunal have jurisdiction to impose all
types of sanction, nor (b) that such jurisdiction ought to be exercised.

[26–27 – 4] Most arbitral rules provide for Party Representatives
(however they are defined) to be identified to the administering
institution and the tribunal itself.[3] Implicit in this is the corollary
that changes must also be notified. It is a small step from here to say
that the change must also be approved expressly (as is found in the
most recent LCIA Rules) or implicitly: Article 18.3 of the LCIA Rules
provides that, following the tribunal's formation, any intended
change or addition by a Party to its representation shall be notified

---

of conduct applicable to the legal profession.' See also: *Reliastar Life Insurance Company of
New York* v. *EMC National Life Company* 564 F.3d 81 (2d Cir. 2009), which held that the
tribunal had power to apportion costs for bad faith conduct notwithstanding a provision that
there was agreement for an even apportionment of costs. In so holding, the Court distin-
guished *InterChem Asia 2000 Pte Ltd* v. *Oceana Petrochemicals AG* 373 F.Supp.2d 340 (SDNY
2005) where the tribunal had sought to sanction counsel directly.

[3] E.g. UNCITRAL Arbitration Rules Art. 5: 'Each party may be represented or assisted by
persons chosen by it. The names and addresses of such persons must be communicated to all
parties and to the arbitral tribunal.' And see Guideline 4.

to the tribunal and 'shall only take effect in the arbitration subject to the approval of the Arbitral Tribunal.'

[26–27 – 5] This provision is clearly aimed at representatives being appointed that would give rise to a conflict with the tribunal (which might be used for tactical reasons so as to create conflict and delay the reference and/or force a resignation from the tribunal). The Party Representative is the agent of the Party, so the LCIA Rule is expressly conferring on the tribunal a power to control who is permitted (and not permitted) to be the authorised agent, for the purposes of the reference, of the Party.

[26–27 – 6] The words in Article 18.3, 'in the arbitration', are intriguing. Clearly, the Rules cannot be aimed at wholly uncon-nected work, such as engaging counsel for wholly unconnected, e.g. M&A, work. It must follow that additional or alternative counsel can be engaged in some capacity provided they are not 'in the arbitra-tion'. Thus counsel who might not be approved by the tribunal (either because the change was not notified to the tribunal – approval was not sought – or because the approval was withheld) might be capable of being engaged purely to advise behind the scenes. The LCIA Rules would seem to prohibit such involvement but the Guidelines would appear to permit this in light of the definition of Party Representative in the Guidelines as one "… who appears in an arbitration on behalf of a Party and makes submissions, arguments or representations to the Arbitral Tribunal on behalf of such Party …". This would permit counsel, who would not be permitted to be a Party Representative, to draft submissions and similarly 'shape' the case.

[26–27 – 7] Thus the approach of the Guidelines is not to prevent a Party appointing counsel – they can appoint whom they wish – and that counsel will be, at least for some purposes, the agent of the Party. Whether that counsel will be permitted to be a Party Representative is, however, another matter. This may mean that disqualification is a fairly pointless exercise. If the issue is one of conflict (as opposed to Misconduct within the reference), an injunction from the relevant state court may be required so as to prevent any form of involvement by the conflicted counsel.

[26–27 – 8] The LCIA method of putting the burden on the Party to justify a change of Party Representative, rather than appointment and challenge under the Guidelines, although perhaps yielding the same net effect, is potentially less aggressive, easier to accept and more efficient than counsel being appointed and subsequently being challenged and potentially disqualified.

Jurisdiction over whom?

[26–27 – 9] The second question is over whom such jurisdiction exists. If it is correct, as it is suggested it is, that the jurisdiction derives from the consent to arbitrate, then it must follow that the primary jurisdiction is over those who have consented to arbitrate: i.e. the Parties rather than counsel or Party Representatives. This is acknowledged by the LCIA Rules – firstly by Article 18.4, where the tribunal has to approve the change in counsel as it is the Party who applies for the change and hence the jurisdiction extends to approving or denying the Party's request. But crucially, Article 18.5 provides that: 'Each party must ensure that all of its legal representatives … have agreed to comply with the general guidelines contained in the Annex … In permitting the legal representative to so appear, a party shall thereby represent that the legal representative has agreed to such compliance.'[4] It seems clear from this that the primary jurisdiction is over the Party.

[26–27 – 10] The discussion under Guidelines 1–3 argues for the possibility of a direct jurisdiction for the tribunal over Party Representatives. If that line of argument is accepted then, in addition to the primary jurisdiction over Parties, there may be a secondary jurisdiction over Party Representatives. As Guideline 26(a) expressly contemplates that the tribunal might exercise a jurisdiction (admonishment) directly over the Party Representative, it is an indication

---

[4] There is no suggestion that a legal representative that is found to have failed to comply with the Guidelines is barred from addressing the tribunal or loses a right of audience (still less that the representative might be barred from representing the Party). The more persuasive argument is that the Party, by agreeing to arbitrate under LCIA Rules, warrants that he will engage representatives who will comply, and hence, if one representative does not comply, the Party warrants that he will engage a representative who will.

that the Guidelines must contemplate some direct jurisdiction over Party Representatives.

[26–27 – 11] Similarly, when it comes to sanctions the LCIA Rules also expressly contemplate sanctions against the Party Representative with a reprimand, caution or other remedy. There is a tension in the LCIA Rules referring, in Articles 18.4 and 18.5, to jurisdiction over the Parties, and Article 18.6 then addresses remedies as being against counsel, but the answer is presumably that Article 18.5 provides that 'Each party shall ensure that all its legal representatives … have agreed to comply with the general guidelines contained in the Annex to the LCIA Rules …' and that paragraph 7 of the Annex to the LCIA Rules provides: 'In accordance with Articles 18.5 and 18.6, the Arbitral Tribunal may decide whether a legal representative has violated these general guidelines and, if so, how to exercise its discretion to impose any or all of the sanctions listed in Article 18.6.'

Due process

[26–27 – 12] Guideline 26 preserves the right of due process (notice and a reasonable opportunity to be heard), but this extends to the Parties and not, expressly, to the Party Representative (it is only the Comments that refers to the *'impugned'* Party Representative – quite why the Guidelines themselves did not refer to the Representative being heard is unclear).[5] The mere reference to due process means that there has to be a 'prosecutor', a 'judge' and a 'jury'. Only the tribunal can fulfil those latter two roles, and that is where the real problems start.

[26–27 – 13] It is to be assumed that the tribunal will be seasoned campaigners with relatively thick skins who will seek to prevent escalation and the invocation of the disciplinary regime under the Guidelines and, especially, Guideline 26. They may cajole and encourage appropriate behaviours and probably warn that inappropriate behaviours should cease before the tribunal considers

---

[5] The extent of the due process is not stated. For example, can the accused Party Representative cross-examine (and what if the primary witness was a tribunal member – e.g. an allegation of improper *ex parte* communication – and can they seek document production)?

more formal measures. It will take something quite outrageous or a series of more minor indiscretions before the 'charge' would be put to the Party Representative by the tribunal – acting as prosecutor. By that stage the tribunal will be fairly persuaded in their own minds that there has been behaviour in breach of one or more Guidelines and that that behaviour should be sanctioned (or at least should be considered for sanction).

[26–27 – 14] It is difficult to see the tribunal fulfilling their role as 'judge' or 'jury' and then dismissing the very 'charge' they put to the Party Representative, and this gives rise to issues of due process and the fairness of the entire sanctioning process.

The alternatives

[26–27 – 15] These are real, practical issues. There are few alternatives to the tribunal undertaking this role themselves: the various 'Courts' – i.e. those established under the institutional rules of the LCIA, ICC etc. – might have fulfilled that role but, certainly in the case of the LCIA, that was considered and rejected. An alternative – which seems to be the only alternative – is for the other Party to act as 'prosecutor'.[6] This is not quite as strange as it might first appear; indeed, the other Party is anticipated to be the primary complainant under LCIA Rules Article 18.6. The other Party is likely to be the victim of any breach of a Guideline, and will be at least as conscious of the breach as anyone else, including the tribunal.[7] Furthermore, it will most likely be the other Party who brings any breach to the attention to the tribunal. In such circumstances it does fall fairly naturally to the other Party to act as 'prosecutor'. In the instances where the tribunal is concerned by behaviours exhibited by a Party Representative it could, relatively easily, draw attention to it and invite the other Party to consider whether a 'charge' should be

[6] The Guidelines do not specify who can and cannot bring a complaint against a Party Representative. By contrast, the LCIA Rules make it clear that it can only be the opposing Party who can do so (Article 18.6).

[7] Although some breaches, e.g. improper *ex parte* communication with the tribunal, will require the tribunal to be, at least, the informant. It is conceivable that a tribunal might announce publicly to the Parties what has transpired and the tribunal might then invite the other Party to consider bringing a complaint for misconduct.

proffered. As soon as that is acknowledged as the process it seems fairly predictable that there would then be charge and counter-charge by the accused Party Representative accusing the other Party Representative of other Misconduct.

Timing

[26–27 – 16] The further practical issue is when any charge should be laid, whether further proceedings should be stayed whilst it is resolved, and whether the Party and its Party Representative consider it appropriate for the Party Representative to continue after any sanction has been imposed. All of these issues may disrupt the reference. Generally, it makes good sense to address issues promptly. Thus, if facts come to light indicating misconduct, the charge should be proffered and the matter investigated and any sanction imposed promptly. Certainly if the potential sanction is the removal of a Party Representative, considerable urgency will often be called for. Indeed, a substantial delay could itself be attacked as tactical and not made in good faith. Under the LCIA Rules it could be argued that a combination of the Preamble and Article 32.1 mean that a failure to raise an objection could amount to a waiver.

[26–27 – 17] Equally, there is no long stop after which the jurisdiction should be exercised, provided, of course, the tribunal is not *functus officio* i.e. has not rendered the final award.

Bias

[26–27 – 18] A further issue is whether, by imposing a sanction (and, it might be said, by proffering a charge and adjudicating upon it), the tribunal has evidenced some bias against a Party and its Party Representative. Tribunals should be careful to avoid any appearance of bias, especially one that might affect the enforceability of the award. Tribunals will therefore be circumspect in making any allegation of Misconduct, the process of decision-making and the language of the decision (which should be as moderate as possible in the circumstances).

[26–27 – 19] Useful guidance might be obtained from *Locabail (UK) Ltd* v. *Bayfield Properties Ltd*,[8] where the court gave guidance as to what challenges on the grounds of bias would and would not be likely to succeed. Challenges based on prior judicial decisions are unlikely to succeed (whether in the same or other cases), as are challenges based on academic writings (unless they go beyond measured debate[9]). A judge who rejects a witness's evidence in outspoken terms may, however, throw doubt on his ability to approach such person's evidence on a future occasion (and hence be a likely basis for challenge); however, mere adverse comment about a Party or witness, or a finding that the evidence of a Party or witness was unreliable, would not, without more justification, found a sustainable objection.[10]

[26–27 – 20] Generally, a judge's prior decisions in a case will not prevent his continuance in later stages unless he expresses himself in such vituperative language that a fair-minded observer would regard him as disqualified.[11]

[26–27 – 21] Wasted or non-Party costs which are analogous to Guidelines 26 and 27 are positively encouraged to be heard by the same judge because of the very familiarity that aids judicial determination. In the infamous case of *Re Freudiana*[12], a case estimated at four weeks took close to a year, and the judge felt that was due to counsel's conduct. Counsel in turn blamed the judge and contended that he should not make that decision. Recognising that another judge could not hear the application proportionately, he dismissed the application that he had initiated for wasted costs.

Sanctions unusual

[26–27 – 22] It is perhaps for these practical reasons, more than any other, that direct sanctions against the Party Representative will be

---

[8] [2000] QB 451.
[9] See *Timmins* v. *Gormley* (dealt with in, and reported as part of, the *Locabail* judgment) where the tone and trenchancy of the views expressed suggested to the reader that the author had fixed and preconceived views.
[10] Although see *Lodwick* v. *Southwark LBC* [2004] EWCA Civ 306.
[11] See e.g. *Sengupta* v. *Holmes* [2006] EWCA Civ 172.   [12] [1994] NPC 89.

extremely rare. The jurisdiction of the tribunal over the Party Representatives is discussed under Guidelines 1–3 above. The extent of that jurisdiction is discussed here.

Proportionality

[26–27 – 23] The Committee Comments to Guidelines 27–28 suggest that the tribunal should seek to apply the most proportionate remedy or combination of remedies in light of the factors listed in Guideline 27, and refer to the process as being *'overarching balancing exercise to be conducted in addressing matters of Misconduct by a Party Representative in order to ensure that the arbitration proceed in a fair and appropriate manner.'* It is clear, therefore, that the aim of the sanction is not to punish *per se* but rather to ensure that (a) the arbitration can and does proceed and (b) that it does so in a proper manner.

[26–27 – 24] In considering Misconduct it must be recalled that Misconduct not only infringes the Guidelines but also whatever the tribunal decides is Misconduct.

Admonishment

[26–27 – 25] In terms of the actual sanction, Guideline 26(a) provides that one of the sanctions that may be imposed is to "admonish" the Party Representative. Presumably, there can be degrees of admonishment from a mild rebuke to a severe reprimand. Tribunals will, no doubt, impose a sanction within that range that is proportionate – in accordance with the Committee Comments. The LCIA Rules provide for a 'written reprimand' or 'written caution'. These sorts of sanction are clearly aimed at the lower end of the scale. Tribunals will, however, be very wary of imposing this type of sanction. This sort of professional discipline is something normally reserved for the local bar/law society or state courts.[13]

---

[13] In contrast, costs sanctions (albeit not typically against Party Representatives) and adverse inferences are much more the territory or jurisdiction of the tribunal. See the discussion below.

[26–27 – 26] A finding of a breach of the Guidelines must logically precede admonishment and reprimand. A caution could be literally that, and caution a Party Representative not to do something in the future, as the LCIA Rules make clear, and there might have been good sense in having the potential of a caution without a finding of breach. However useful that might have been, the LCIA Rules make it clear that the caution that the Rules contemplate is made after a breach (or violation, as the LCIA Rules term it). Nevertheless, even where the tribunal finds no breach, a caution regarding future behaviour might have a salutary effect (but for the reasons discussed here it would be preferable not to make it a formal sanction).

Inferences

[26–27 – 27] Guideline 26(b) provides for inferences (presumably adverse) to be drawn in assessing evidence (whether factual or expert) or legal arguments. Although not expressly stated in the Guideline, there must presumably be a causative link between the Misconduct and the sanction contemplated or imposed. Thus, if unreasonable or excessive fees have been paid to a witness (a breach of Guideline 25), it may well be appropriate to draw an adverse inference on the evidence of that witness but it would be unlikely to be appropriate to draw any adverse inference to unconnected expert evidence. The inference may be more likely the more heinous the Misconduct, e.g. if there is a breach of Guideline 23 and the Party Representative has encouraged false evidence.

[26–27 – 28] As discussed above, Guideline 9: "A Party Representative should not make any knowingly false submission of fact to the Arbitral Tribunal" relates purely to facts rather than legal arguments (although the Committee Comments state that only legal arguments that are subjectively reasonable should be advanced). Quite how it is envisaged that (assuming the Committee Comments to have the force of the Guideline) the tribunal discovers the Party Representative has no subjective belief in the reasonableness of the legal arguments he is making is unclear. Presumably it will be because the tribunal is utterly unpersuaded by the argument, but it will be an extreme scenario where the Party Representative confesses that he has no belief in the argument he advances – as the duty to the client will prevent this admission. If the tribunal is utterly unpersuaded, there is logically no need to draw an inference that it is hopeless – at least on that submission.

[26–27 – 29] The tribunal might, however, be tempted to draw the inference that other potentially sound submissions should be inferred to be weak (or hopeless). That is a dangerous course to follow. Counsel will often make a mixed bag of submissions, conscious that some tribunals like to give something to both sides (the so-called 'splitting of the baby'), and for the tribunal to taint the good with the bad means that counsel must only make good arguments. That would be contrary to the Party Representative's overriding duty to the Party he represents and contrary to the primary duty of loyalty recognised in Guideline 3. Drawing inferences on legal arguments is dangerous and is unlikely to be appropriate; it is a power that should be exercised with extreme caution.

[26–27 – 30] The Guidelines further provide that the tribunal "draw appropriate inferences in assessing the evidence relied upon". This is not particularly apt for evidence that is not on the record but ought to have been – i.e. evidence destroyed or withheld by the Party Representative. One might have thought that the absence of evidence is something that might be particularly suited to the drawing of inferences. If this difficulty in the language of the Guideline can be overcome, there are a number of further difficulties such as whether the Party was complicit in the destruction or withholding of evidence: if the Party asserts its innocence (and the tribunal accepts that), an adverse inference may be inappropriate.

[26–27 – 31] On the other hand, if a Party fails to call a particular witness whose evidence is conspicuous by its absence, the tribunal might well consider an inference (see IBA Rules Article 9(6)[14]), but these are unlikely to be due to Party Representative Misconduct.

[26–27 – 32] It is to be noted that the drawing of adverse inferences is not a sanction available under the LCIA Rules because, under Article 18.6 of those Rules, the sanction has to be against the counsel

[14] And see IBA Rules Article 9(5) relating to documents not adduced.

and not the Party. The tribunal will, however, be perfectly entitled to weigh the evidence and consider the submissions, taking all matters into account, and may well arrive at the same place by a different route.[15]

Costs

[26–27 – 33] If a sanction is called for, penalising a Party in costs, as provided for in Guideline 26(c), is the most likely sanction and one already used by tribunals on a reasonably regular basis.[16] A sanction in costs for a misconceived legal argument is far more likely to be an appropriate way to proceed than admonishing the Party Representative. A misconceived legal argument may impact on time and costs but is unlikely, if identified (which it must be assumed to be), to impact on the fairness and integrity of the process. It has been recognised for what it is and, presumably, dismissed. The time and cost can be compensated in costs. Similarly, for false or irrelevant evidence, which again is to be assumed as having been identified as unreliable, the appropriate sanction will often be in costs.

[26–27 – 34] The ability for the tribunal to indicate that a specific part of the costs are attributable to a Party Representative's conduct is a coercive measure. It does not detract from the liability of the Party for such costs but it does permit the Party to say to its Party Representative that it should carry that liability (and some tribunals have reportedly gone as far as to say that, although the liability is that of the Party, it encourages the Party Representative to pay or reimburse the Party). If, however, the discussion under Guidelines 1–3 is correct and the tribunal does have jurisdiction over Party Representatives as the agent of the Party then a costs order could be made directly against the Party Representative.

---

[15] Note that adverse inferences may also be drawn under Articles 9.5 (failure to produce a document) and 9.6 (failure to adduce any other evidence including testimony) of the IBA Rules, and note that Article 9.7 also provides that any failure by a Party to conduct itself in good faith in the taking of evidence permits the tribunal to reflect that in costs in addition to 'any other measures available under these Rules'.

[16] Hence the tribunal will be familiar with the exercise of the jurisdiction and, as the costs discretion is wide, a tribunal might well be influenced by matters that might be Misconduct in making a costs order or award, albeit whilst not formally imposing a sanction. Note IBA Rules Article 9(7).

[26–27 – 35] Again, note that costs sanctions are not available against a Party Representative under the LCIA Rules as these are only permissible against the Party.

Other sanctions

[26–27 – 36] The catch-all of the tribunal taking any other appropriate measure in order to preserve the fairness and integrity of the proceedings provided for in Guideline 26(d) leaves open a wide discretion.

[26–27 – 37] Article 18.6 of the LCIA Rules has a slightly more expansive wording permitting any other measure provided it is necessary to fulfil the general duties of the tribunal, so as to (i) act fairly and impartially, (ii) grant a reasonable opportunity to be heard, (iii) avoid unnecessary delay and expense, and (iv) provide a fair, efficient and expeditious resolution.

Removal/disqualification of counsel

[26–27 – 38] The potential range of sanctions is, presumably, considerable[17], but the clear 'elephant in the room' is the sanction of removing counsel. Such removal is not the same as preventing the Party from instructing that counsel as (one of the) Party Representative(s) or otherwise seeking to prevent the involvement of that counsel.

[26–27 – 39] The issue of disqualifying counsel came to the forefront of many people's minds with two ICSID cases: *Hrvatska Elektropivreda d.d.* v. *Republic of Slovenia*[18] and *Rompetrol Group NV* v. *Romania*[19].

[26–27 – 40] In *Hrvatska*, some two years after the tribunal had been appointed and ten days before the substantive evidentiary hearing,

---

[17] Examples might include excluding from evidence or production any document, statement or oral testimony (c.f. IBA Rules Article 9(2)); an adjournment; and the drawing of adverse inferences (c.f. IBA Rules Articles 9(5) & (6)).
[18] ICSID Case No. ARB/05/24 6 May 2008.
[19] ICSID Case No. ARB/06/3 14 January 2010.

the respondent sought to add a counsel who was affiliated with the chambers of the president of the tribunal. The claimant sought an order that the respondent 'refrain from using the services of' the new counsel on the basis that there was a justifiable doubt as to the independence of the president – on the basis that the English chambers system was wholly foreign to the claimant and its Party Representative. The application was put on the familiar basis of (lack of) independence of tribunal members. The parties agreed that they did not want the president to stand down for obvious cost and delay reasons.

[26–27 – 41] The tribunal found that the parties in an arbitral procedure 'as a general rule [...] may seek such representation as they see fit'.[20] However, the tribunal found that this general rule is overridden by the principle of the 'immutability of properly constituted tribunal'.[21] The tribunal ruled that the barrister 'may not participate further as counsel in this case'.[22]

[26–27 – 42] The tribunal took several aspects into consideration; it argued that 'it seems unacceptable for the solution to reside in the individual national bodies which regulate the work of professional service providers, because that might lead to inconsistent or indeed arbitrary outcomes depending on the attitudes of such bodies, or the content (or lack of relevant content) of their rules. It would moreover be disruptive to interrupt international cases to ascertain the position taken by such bodies.'[23]

[26–27 – 43] The tribunal went on to observe that 'there is an "inherent power of an international court to deal with any issues necessary for the conduct of matters falling within its jurisdiction"; that power "exists independently of any statutory reference". In the specific circumstances of the present case, it is in the Tribunal's view both necessary and appropriate to take action under its inherent power.'[24]

[26–27 – 44] The tribunal found the objection 'well founded' and ordered that the new counsel 'may not participate further as counsel in this case'.

---

[20] *Hrvatska* at [24].   [21] *Ibid.* at [25].   [22] *Ibid.* at [Ruling 1].   [23] *Ibid.* at [23].
[24] *Ibid.* at [33].

[26–27 – 45] The decision is not the easiest to follow, but it appears that the tribunal accepted that (a) the standard for disqualification of counsel was the same as if an application had been made to remove a member of the tribunal, and (b) that that standard was satisfied.[25] But it appears from the reasoning of the tribunal that that, of itself, would not have been sufficient and it was only because it was supplemented by the failure to adequately disclose the connection. Among the particular features of this failure were: a 'conscious decision not to inform' the tribunal; the tardiness in notifying; and an 'insistent refusal to discuss the scope' of the new counsel's involvement. All these may have been 'errors of judgment' but they created 'an atmosphere of apprehension and mistrust which it was important to dispel'.[26]

[26–27 – 46] By contrast, in *Rompetrol* v. *Romania*[27] the tribunal noted that it would be incorrect to attribute the power to remove to the tribunal but it was willing to 'assume' that there were such powers but that any such power should only be exercised under 'extraordinary circumstances, these being circumstances which genuinely touch on the integrity of the arbitral process as assessed by the Tribunal itself'.[28] On the request to disqualify the claimant counsel who had, for four years – and until seven months previously – been in the same firm as the claimant's party appointed arbitrator, the tribunal observed that 'a power on the part of a judicial tribunal of any kind to exercise a control over the representation of the parties in proceedings before it is by definition a weighty instrument, the more so if the proposition is that the control ought to be exercised by excluding or overriding a party's own choice'.[29] Whilst affirming its authority to rely on the *Hrvatska* doctrine, the tribunal refused to disqualify counsel, arguing 'the only justification for such extension in the arbitral context would be a clear need to safeguard the essential integrity of the arbitral process, on the basis that such integrity

---

[25] It is important to have firmly in mind that there will be instances where the putative arbitrator must disclose connections, but those may well not necessitate withdrawal or disqualification. See e.g. IBA Guidelines on Conflicts.
[26] *Ibid.* at [31].
[27] *Rompetrol Group N.V.* v. *Romania*, ICSID Case No. ARB/06/3, 14 January 2010.
[28] *Ibid.* at [15].   [29] *Ibid.* at [16].

would be compromised were the exclusion not ordered'.[30] No such circumstances were found to exist as no 'risk ... genuinely exist[ed]' that the integrity of the tribunal would be affected.

[26–27 – 47] The *Rompetrol* tribunal characterised the *Hrvatska* decision as 'an ad hoc sanction for the failure to make proper disclosure in good time' rather than a holding of more general application. Underlying the decision was the clear finding that the presence of the new counsel would not (or, at least, not seriously) affect the neutrality of the tribunal.[31]

[26–27 – 48] The willingness of other ICSID tribunals to consider the disqualification of counsel in other circumstances can be seen in *Libananco Holdings Co. v. Turkey*[32] and *Fraport AG Frankfurt Airport Services Worldwide v. Repulic of the Philippines*.[33] In the former the tribunal declared with respect to misconduct that 'if instructions [to counsel] have been given with the benefit of improperly obtained privileged or confidential information, severe prejudice may result. If that event arises, the Tribunal may consider other remedies available apart from the exclusion of improperly obtained evidence or information.'[34] In the latter the respondent sought to remove claimant's counsel on the grounds that he had represented the respondent in a prior (and linked) ICC arbitration. The tribunal quite correctly disclaimed any deontological responsibility – it made it plain that its only task was to ensure the fairness and integrity of the process. The tribunal was not swayed by the relevant bar rules (although it asked to be briefed on them) for some common general principles and any remedy was to address any perceived harm only – on the facts it found no risk that needed to be addressed.

[26–27 – 49] Those who object to the disqualification of counsel usually rely upon the right to engage counsel of choice; however, the right to counsel of your choice is only one element of fair proceedings. Where there is conflict of interest or perceived or potential conflict between counsel and the tribunal or a member of it, the right

---

[30] *Ibid.* at [22].   [31] *Ibid.* at [15], [18] and [26].
[32] ICSID Case No. ARB/06/8 23 June 2008.
[33] ICSID Case. No. ARB/03/25 18 September 2008.   [34] *Libananco* at [80].

to choose counsel must, however, yield to having an independent tribunal as being a more fundamental right.[35]

[26–27 – 50] The freedom of the Parties to be represented by counsel of their own choice is a fundamental element of international arbitration, such that Parties may be represented by anyone of their choice, whether or not a lawyer.[36] This can be seen as an aspect of Model Law Art. 18: 'The parties shall be treated with equality and each party shall be given a full opportunity of presenting its case.'

[26–27 – 51] The Guidelines reflect this freedom, defining Representative as

any person [...] who appears in an arbitration on behalf of a Party and makes submissions, arguments or representations to the Arbitral Tribunal on behalf of such Party, other than in the capacity as a Witness or Expert, and whether or not legally qualified or admitted to a Domestic Bar.

[26–27 – 52] The right to be represented by counsel of choice can potentially come into conflict with the right to efficient and effective arbitral proceedings. The tribunal has the duty and the responsibility to oversee and adjudicate over the arbitral proceedings that necessarily comprises the Parties' presentation of their cases.

[26–27 – 53] The consequences arising from a tribunal's possible competence to remove counsel is 'draconian'[37] because it deprives the Parties of the right to be represented by counsel of their choice. This deprivation would not only shatter this fundamental right in

---

[35] The proposition that the tribunal have jurisdiction can be tested by postulating a Party Representative who seeks to bribe, or physically assaults, the tribunal. Continued representation must surely be nigh on impossible.

[36] See e.g.: Section 36 of the English Arbitration Act 1996: 'Unless otherwise agreed by the parties, a party to arbitral proceedings may be represented in the proceedings by a lawyer or other person chosen by him.' UNCITRAL Rules, Art. 5: 'Each party may be represented or assisted by persons chosen by it'; ICSID Arbitration Rules R.18 'Each party may be represented or assisted by agents, counsel or advocates whose names and authority shall be notified to the Secretary-General ...'; LCIA Rules, Art. 18(1): 'Any party may be represented by legal practitioners or any other representatives'; WIPO Rules, Art. 13(a): 'The parties may be represented by persons of their choice, irrespective of, in particular, nationality or professional qualification'; CIETAC Rules, Art. 20.

[37] Rau A.S. (2014) Arbitrators Without Powers? Disqualifying Counsel, *Arbitral Proceedings*. 2014, pp. 9–10. Available: http://ssrn.com/abstract=2403054 [consulted 22 May 2015].

international arbitration but would also likely violate the New York Convention.

[26–27 – 54] Only in rare cases will the applicable law or the arbitration agreement explicitly prohibit a disqualification of counsel.[38] In any case of disqualification contrary to law, any subsequent award may well not be recognised based on Article VI(d) of the New York Convention.

[26–27 – 55] But there are some exceptions to these principles where arbitral tribunals might be able to remove counsel from further representation in the arbitration: for example, when counsel has some sort of relationship with a member of the tribunal such as to amount to a conflict of interest.[39] This is the only context in which the possibility of disqualification is directly addressed in the IBA Guidelines:

> *The Arbitral Tribunal may, in case of breach of Guideline 5, take measures appropriate to safeguard the integrity of the proceedings, including the exclusion of the new Party Representative from participating in all or part of the arbitral proceedings.*[40]

[26–27 – 56] This raises the question as to which situations are comprised by the definition of *'compelling circumstances'*[41] in which a tribunal may order a Party to dismiss counsel or terminate its representation. It is unlikely that a tribunal in a commercial arbitration would use lower standards than the tribunals in the above-mentioned ICSID cases, bearing in mind that excluding counsel would be likely to form the basis for a challenge to an award or to its enforcement. However, following the Guidelines, disqualification is expressly possible and justified if counsel has joined the proceedings for the purpose or with the consequence of creating a conflict of interest. It remains to be seen to what extent tribunals use inherent powers "to ensure the integrity and fairness of the arbitral proceedings"[42] to disqualify counsel from the proceedings and

---

[38] The only known case is the German Code of Civil Procedure, which contains a mandatory rule that prohibits a tribunal from disqualifying lawyers (Section 1042 of the German Code of Civil procedure). Available at http://www.dis-arb.de/de/51/materialien/german-arbitration-law-98-id3 (accessed 5 October 2015).

[39] See Guideline 5.   [40] Guideline 6.

[41] In the words of the Committee Comments to Guidelines 5 and 6.   [42] Guideline 1.

thereby undermine the Party's right to a free and unfettered choice of counsel. Such a result appears to be most likely in cases where counsel is involved in especially obstructive conduct, particularly without approval by (or, perhaps, notice to) the Party he represents.

[26–27 – 57] Both the Guidelines and the LCIA Rules specifically provide for change of counsel or the introduction of new counsel after the proceedings have commenced in a manner that might potentially disrupt a fair hearing. A mere change should assume an attempt to affect the integrity of the process and a challenge.

[26–27 – 58] The approach of the Guidelines, Guidelines 4–6, authorises a tribunal to exclude a new Party Representative from participating in proceedings if to do so would safeguard the integrity of the proceedings. Thus, to be excluded or refused permission to participate, there must be compelling evidence and not merely speculation that the Party Representative would affect the integrity of the process. Clearly, in the case of an objective conflict, this will be more readily evidenced than, for example, a tendency to disrupt.

Due process and confidentiality owed to client

[26–27 – 59] Insofar as the tribunal considers a remedy against a Party Representative it will have to bear in mind that the Party Representative may be unable to defend himself as part of an intended defence may involve the use of privileged material. For instance, a Party Representative may have advised that the legal argument is hopeless[43] but have been instructed to argue it nevertheless. As with any other application for whatever relief against a Party Representative, great care needs to be exercised.[44]

---

[43] Leaving to one side Guideline 9 and the Committee Comment: *'With respect to legal submissions to the Tribunal, a Party Representative may argue any construction of a law, a contract, a treaty or any authority that he or she believes is reasonable.'*

[44] See generally *Medcalf* v. *Mardell* [2002] 3 All ER 721. The case concerned a wasted costs application against counsel. Counsel had settled a court document and a skeleton argument making serious allegations of impropriety. Counsel argued that they had credible material before them to make the allegations (as required by the Bar rules). The client had refused to waive privilege to the documents and hence counsel could not demonstrate that they had complied with their obligations. The court held that it must be slow to conclude that counsel did not have sufficient material to justify his conduct. They were entitled to the benefit of the doubt. The court should not make a wasted costs order without satisfying

The form of the sanction

[26–27 – 60] The form of any sanction is not specified in the Guidelines. It seems likely that any sanction will take the form of a procedural order (although cost sanctions, in particular, may be included in an award). Furthermore, the Guidelines are silent as to whether any decision should be reasoned, but it is very clear that any such order (especially one imposing sanctions) should be fully reasoned. The spectre of imposing sanctions is likely to give to subsequent perceptions or allegations of bias, and a fully reasoned procedural order will go a long way to reducing the perception of bias and will enable any subsequent court review or appeal to fully understand what the tribunal did and why.

[26–17 – 61] Equally, it may be appropriate for the tribunal to explain any remedial action that the tribunal took or ordered so as to again help any reviewing court. For example, if a Party Representative was found guilty of suppressing documents, the tribunal could either take direct steps to have the documents produced or continue without them. The latter is particularly possible if the suppression were found out during the course of a final evidentiary hearing and producing the documents might cause substantial delay and cost if the evidentiary hearing had to be adjourned.

An enforceable award

[26–17 – 62] The tribunal will want to make an enforceable award. If, for example, a Party Representative were removed, the aggrieved Party might well complain that it was deprived of counsel of its choice. In England the challenge to the award would be under s.68 Arbitration Act 1996 that the award was arrived at after a serious irregularity causing substantial prejudice. At the very least this would

---

itself that it was fair to do so, and the refusal to waive privilege made it unfair to reach a conclusion that counsel had no credible material upon which to base the allegation. Only exceptionally could those exacting conditions be satisfied and the power should not be used so as to impinge on the contribution that an advocate made to the administration of justice. As Lord Steyn said: 'Making allegations of dishonesty without adequate grounds for doing so may be improper conduct. Not making allegations of dishonesty where it is proper to make such allegations may amount to dereliction of duty.'

be seriously arguable, and is another reason why, notwithstanding the jurisdiction, tribunals will be very hesitant about exercising it.

Confidentiality

[26–27 – 63] Any procedural order (and even an award) would remain confidential and hence would not be published (save in ICSID cases). Three issues arise: firstly, whether a tribunal could send a copy of the procedural order or a redacted form of it to the Party Representative's professional body (local bar or Law Society);[45] and, secondly, whether redacted and anonymised findings might be published to indicate 'norms' of unacceptable behaviour; and, thirdly, whether one of the generally accepted exceptions to confidentiality applies.

[26–27 – 64] Arbitral confidentiality is not absolute. It is well established that there exceptions.[46] Two such exceptions are (i) where it is reasonably necessary for the protection of the legitimate interests of an arbitrating party, and (ii) where the interests of justice require disclosure and (perhaps) where the public interest requires disclosure. This may arguably cover the potential for the tribunal to breach arbitral confidentiality. If there is a pending arbitration, as there must be for the tribunal to be considering the issue, the power to authorise what would otherwise be a breach of confidentiality rests, as between the parties and the tribunal, with the tribunal.[47] It would, however, be quite a dramatic step for the tribunal to breach

---

[45] Earlier drafts of the LCIA Rules had the express power to report to the Party Representative's local bar or Law Society. This was dropped in the final draft. Reporting has a number of difficulties: (1) identifying the correct bar etc. if the Representative is a member of more than one bar; (2) maintaining the confidentiality of the arbitration; (3) whether issues of privilege prevent a fair hearing; (4) whether any finding of fact and imposition of sanction is sufficiently robust; and (5) whether reporting is necessary (a requirement of the LCIA Rules but not the Guidelines – although in practice tribunals, governed by the Guidelines, are likely to do only what is necessary) to maintain the fairness and integrity of the arbitration: it seems unlikely that reporting will result in sufficiently rapid action that it impact at all on the arbitration.

[46] See e.g. *Hassneh Insurance Co of Israel* v. *Mew* [1993] 2 Lloyds Rep 243; *Department of Economic Policy and Development of the City of Moscow* v. *Bankers Trust Co.* [2004] EWCA Civ 314; *Ali Shipping Corp* v. *Shipyard Trogir* [2007] EWCA Civ 3054; and *Emmott* v. *Michael Wilson & Partners* [2008] EWCA Civ 184.

[47] In a different context, see the discussion in *Emmott* op. cit. at [123].

arbitral confidentiality in any circumstances, and – absent something most unusual – the Party instructing the Party Representative is unlikely to consent to waive arbitral confidentiality, so irrespective of whatever jurisdiction the tribunal has over the Party Representative, it is most unlikely that the tribunal will make a reference to a local bar or Law Society that would involve a breach of confidentiality without consent.[48]

[26–27 – 65] The existence of confidentiality may mean that the Party Representative is more willing than it would be in a state court to risk reputational damage (and potentially costs). That is an unfortunate consequence of confidentiality but no reason to dispense with confidentiality or breach the obligation.

Conclusion of sanctions

[26–27 – 66] It is suggested that the imposition of sanctions will be very rare as the conduct that might invite sanctions is itself rare and the hurdles to any imposition are considerable. The most likely sanction, rather strangely, is the one that is not expressly mentioned: the removal or disqualification of a Party Representative. Rather than actually being used, it is likely that the mere existence of the Guidelines and the mention of them by a tribunal will have a coercive effect and Party Representatives will think more carefully about potentially abusive conduct. The likelihood of formal admonishment, adverse inferences or costs is small, but that is not to say that a tribunal will not warn and cajole to obtain a proper standard of behaviour, will not assess all evidence and submissions in the round and allocate costs as they see fit without making those "sanctions" expressly against a Party Representative rather than the Party.

---

[48] The proposition can be tested by supposing the Party Representative was sanctioned and sought to clear his name by some sort of declaratory application to his professional body or otherwise. The Party Representative would wish to rely on confidential papers in the arbitration. The Party Representative is bound by the same confidentiality as a Party. The Party Representative might have his own rights to a free and impartial hearing, and as it will not have agreed to have its claims resolved by the agreement to arbitrate, any refusal of permission by the tribunal to use arbitration papers may infringe such rights: see generally *Webb* v. *Lewis Silkin* [2015] EWHC 687(Ch).

Extract from the LCIA Arbitration Rules 2014

ARTICLE 18 LEGAL REPRESENTATIVES

18.1 Any party may be represented in the arbitration by one or more authorised legal representatives appearing by name before the Arbitral Tribunal.

18.2 Until the Arbitral Tribunal's formation, the Registrar may request from any party: (i) written proof of the authority granted by that party to any legal representative designated in its Request or Response; and (ii) written confirmation of the names and addresses of all such party's legal representatives in the arbitration. After its formation, at any time, the Arbitral Tribunal may order any party to provide similar proof or confirmation in any form it considers appropriate.

18.3 Following the Arbitral Tribunal's formation, any intended change or addition by a party to its legal representatives shall be notified promptly in writing to all other parties, the Arbitral Tribunal and the Registrar; and any such intended change or addition shall only take effect in the arbitration subject to the approval of the Arbitral Tribunal.

18.4 The Arbitral Tribunal may withhold approval of any intended change or addition to a party's legal representatives where such change or addition could compromise the composition of the Arbitral Tribunal or the finality of any award (on the grounds of possible conflict or other like impediment). In deciding whether to grant or withhold such approval, the Arbitral Tribunal shall have regard to the circumstances, including: the general principle that a party may be represented by a legal representative chosen by that party, the stage which the arbitration has reached, the efficiency resulting from maintaining the composition of the Arbitral Tribunal (as constituted throughout the arbitration) and any likely wasted costs or loss of time resulting from such change or addition.

18.5 Each party shall ensure that all its legal representatives appearing by name before the Arbitral Tribunal have agreed to comply with the general guidelines contained in the Annex to the LCIA Rules, as a condition of such representation. In permitting any legal representative so to appear, a party shall thereby represent that the legal representative has agreed to such compliance.

18.6 In the event of a complaint by one party against another party's legal representative appearing by name before the Arbitral Tribunal (or of such complaint by the Arbitral Tribunal upon its own initiative), the Arbitral Tribunal may decide, after consulting the parties and granting that legal representative a reasonable opportunity to answer the complaint, whether or not the legal representative has violated the general guidelines. If such violation is found by the Arbitral Tribunal, the Arbitral Tribunal may order any or all of the following sanctions against the legal representative: (i) a written reprimand; (ii) a written caution as to future conduct in the arbitration; and (iii) any other measure necessary to fulfil within the arbitration the general duties required of the Arbitral Tribunal under Articles 14.4(i) and (ii).

ANNEX TO THE LCIA RULES

General Guidelines for the Parties' Legal Representatives

(Articles 18.5 and 18.6 of the LCIA Rules)

Paragraph 1: These general guidelines are intended to promote the good and equal conduct of the parties' legal representatives appearing by name within the arbitration. Nothing in these guidelines is intended to derogate from the Arbitration Agreement or to undermine any legal representative's primary duty of loyalty to the party represented in the arbitration or the obligation to present that party's case effectively to the Arbitral Tribunal. Nor shall these guidelines derogate from any mandatory laws, rules of law, professional rules or codes of conduct if and to the extent that any are shown to apply to a legal representative appearing in the arbitration.

Paragraph 2: A legal representative should not engage in activities intended unfairly to obstruct the arbitration or to jeopardise the finality of any award, including repeated challenges to an arbitrator's appointment or to the jurisdiction or authority of the Arbitral Tribunal known to be unfounded by that legal representative.

Paragraph 3: A legal representative should not knowingly make any false statement to the Arbitral Tribunal or the LCIA Court.

Paragraph 4: A legal representative should not knowingly procure or assist in the preparation of or rely upon any false evidence presented to the Arbitral Tribunal or the LCIA Court.

Paragraph 5: A legal representative should not knowingly conceal or assist in the concealment of any document (or any part thereof) which is ordered to be produced by the Arbitral Tribunal.

Paragraph 6: During the arbitration proceedings, a legal representative should not deliberately initiate or attempt to initiate with any member of the Arbitral Tribunal or with any member of the LCIA Court making any determination or decision in regard to the arbitration (but not including the Registrar) any unilateral contact relating to the arbitration or the parties' dispute, which has not been disclosed in writing prior to or shortly after the time of such contact to all other parties, all members of the Arbitral Tribunal (if comprised of more than one arbitrator) and the Registrar in accordance with Article 13.4.

Paragraph 7: In accordance with Articles 18.5 and 18.6, the Arbitral Tribunal may decide whether a legal representative has violated these general guidelines and, if so, how to exercise its discretion to impose any or all of the sanctions listed in Article 18.6.

Interaction of IBA Rules with major professional conduct rules

IBA Guidelines on Party Representation 2013	ABA Model Rules of Professional Conduct 2013	Bar Standards Board Handbook (England and Wales) 2015 and Solicitors Regulation Authority (SRA) Code of Conduct 2011	Rules of Professional Conduct of the Swiss Bar Association 2005	Singapore Legal Profession (Professional Conduct) Rules 2012	Australian Solicitor Conduct Rules 2012	Council of Bars and Law Societies of Europe (CCBE) Code of Conduct 2013
Candour and honesty						
A party representative should not make any knowingly false submission of fact to the arbitral tribunal (Guideline 9). A party representative should not submit witness or expert evidence that he or she knows to be false (Guideline 11).	A lawyer shall not knowingly make a false statement of fact or law to a tribunal or fail to correct a false statement of material fact or law previously made to the tribunal by the lawyer (Rule 3.3 (a)(1)). A lawyer shall not knowingly fail to disclose to the tribunal legal authority in the controlling jurisdiction known to the lawyer to be directly adverse to the position of the client and not disclosed by opposing counsel (Rule 3.3 (a)(2)).	A barrister has an overriding duty to act with independence in the interests of justice. He must assist the court in the administration of justice and must not deceive or knowingly or recklessly mislead the court (Bar Standards rC3.1; rC6). A barrister must not knowingly or recklessly mislead or attempt to mislead anyone else (Bar Standards rC9.1). A solicitor should not attempt to deceive or knowingly or recklessly mislead	A party representative should refrain from everything which could put his trustworthiness into question (Article 1).	An advocate and solicitor shall at all times act with due courtesy to the court before which he is appearing (Rule 55 (a)). An advocate and solicitor shall not knowingly deceive or mislead the court, any other advocate and solicitor, witness, court officer, or other person or body involved in or associated with court proceedings (Rule 56).	A solicitor must not deceive or knowingly or recklessly mislead the court (Rule 19.1). But he will not have made a misleading statement to a court simply by failing to correct an error in a statement made to the court by the opponent or any other person (Rule 19.3). A solicitor must not knowingly make a false statement to an opponent in relation to the case (Rule 22.1). A solicitor must not engage in conduct, in the course of	A lawyer shall while maintaining due respect and courtesy towards the court defend the interests of the client honourably and fearlessly without regard to the lawyer's own interests or to any consequences to him- or herself or to any other person (Article 4.3). A lawyer shall never knowingly give false or misleading information to the court (Article 4.4).

IBA Guidelines on Party Representation 2013	ABA Model Rules of Professional Conduct 2013	Bar Standards Board Handbook (England and Wales) 2015 and Solicitors Regulation Authority (SRA) Code of Conduct 2011	Rules of Professional Conduct of the Swiss Bar Association 2005	Singapore Legal Profession (Professional Conduct) Rules 2012	Australian Solicitor Conduct Rules 2012	Council of Bars and Law Societies of Europe (CCBE) Code of Conduct 2013
	A lawyer shall not knowingly offer evidence that the lawyer knows to be false. If a lawyer, the lawyer's client, or a witness called by the lawyer, has offered material evidence and the lawyer comes to know of its falsity, the lawyer shall take reasonable remedial measures, including, if necessary, disclosure to the tribunal (Rule 3.3 (a)(3)).	the court (SRA Outcome 5.1). A solicitor must draw the court's attention to relevant cases and statutory provisions (SRA Indicative Behaviour 5.2). A solicitor must immediately inform the court, with the client's consent, if during the course of proceedings he becomes aware that he has inadvertently misled the court, or ceasing to act if the client does not consent to inform the court (SRA Indicative Behaviour 5.4).			practice or otherwise, which demonstrates that the solicitor is not a fit and proper person to practise law (Rule 5.1).	The rules governing a lawyer's relations with the courts apply also to the lawyer's relations with arbitrators and any other persons exercising judicial or quasi-judicial functions, even on an occasional basis (Article 4.5).

Communication with court/tribunal

Unless agreed otherwise by the parties, a party representative should not engage in any ex	In an ex parte proceeding, a lawyer shall inform the tribunal of all	There are no prescribed rules of this sort of court communication	A lawyer must not submit to the court any proposals for settlement of the	An advocate and solicitor representing an interested party	A solicitor must not, outside an ex parte application or a hearing of which	The lawyer must not make contact with the judge without first

informing the lawyer acting for the opposing party or submit exhibits, notes or documents to the judge without communicating them in good time to the lawyer on the other side unless such steps are permitted under the relevant rules of procedure. To the extent not prohibited by law a lawyer must not divulge or submit to the court any proposals for settlement of the case made by the other party or its lawyer without the express consent of the other party's lawyer. (Commentary on Article 4.2).

an opponent has had proper notice, communicate in the opponent's absence with the court concerning any matter of substance in connection with current proceedings (Rule 22.5).

shall not initiate communication with the court about the facts, issues or any other matter in a case that the advocate and solicitor knows is pending or likely to be pending before the court unless the advocate and solicitor has first informed the persons acting for all other interested parties of the nature of the matters he wishes to communicate with the court and has given them an opportunity to be present or to reply (Rule 63 (1)).

case made by the other party or its lawyer without the express consent of the other party's lawyer (Article 6).

neither in the Bar Standards Board Handbook nor in the SRA Code of Conduct.

material facts known to the lawyer that will enable the tribunal to make an informed decision, whether or not the facts are adverse (Rule 3.3 (d)).

parte communications with an arbitrator concerning the arbitration (Guideline 7).

IBA Guidelines on Party Representation 2013	ABA Model Rules of Professional Conduct 2013	Bar Standards Board Handbook (England and Wales) 2015 and Solicitors Regulation Authority (SRA) Code of Conduct 2011	Rules of Professional Conduct of the Swiss Bar Association 2005	Singapore Legal Profession (Professional Conduct) Rules 2012	Australian Solicitor Conduct Rules 2012	Council of Bars and Law Societies of Europe (CCBE) Code of Conduct 2013
Information exchange and disclosure						
The party representative should inform the client of the need to preserve, so far as reasonably possible, relevant documents (Guideline 12). A party representative should not make any request to produce, or any objection to a request to produce, for an improper purpose, such as to harass or cause unnecessary delay (Guideline 13). A party representative should not suppress or conceal, or advise a party to suppress or conceal, documents that have been requested by another	A lawyer shall not in pre-trial procedure, make a frivolous discovery request or fail to make reasonably diligent effort to comply with a legally proper discovery request by an opposing party (Rule 3.4(d)). A lawyer shall not unlawfully obstruct another party's access to evidence or unlawfully alter, destroy or conceal a document or other material having potential evidentiary value. A lawyer shall not counsel or assist another person to do any such act (Rule 3.4 (a)).	A barrister must take reasonable steps to avoid wasting the court's time (Bar Standards rC3.3).	There are no prescribed rules of information exchange and disclosure in the Swiss Rules of Professional Conduct.	An advocate and solicitor shall use his best endeavours to avoid unnecessary adjournments, expense and waste of the Court's time (Rule 55 (b)).	A solicitor must not disclose any information which is confidential to a client and acquired by the solicitor during the client's engagement (Rule 9.1). This is subject to multiple exceptions (Rules 9.2.1 – 9.2.6) e.g. if the solicitor is permitted or is compelled by law to disclose (Rule 9.2.2). A solicitor who, as a result of information provided by the client or a witness called on behalf of the client, learns	There are no prescribed rules of information exchange and disclosure in the CCBE Code of Conduct.

Witness/Experts interviews and preparation

IBA	ABA Model Rules	Bar Standards	Swiss	Singapore	SRA	CCBE
party or that the party whom he or she represents has undertaken, or been ordered, to produce (Guideline 16).					that the client or a witness called on behalf of the client has suppressed or procured another person to suppress material evidence upon a topic where there was a positive duty to make disclosure to the court must advise the client that the court should be informed of the lie, falsification or suppression and request authority so to inform the court (Rule 20.1.4).	There are no prescribed rules of witness/expert interviews and preparation in the CCBE Code of Conduct.
A party representative should seek to ensure that a witness statement reflects the witness's own account of relevant facts, events and circumstances (Guideline 21). A party representative should seek to ensure	A lawyer shall not falsify evidence, counsel or assist a witness to testify falsely, or offer an inducement to a witness that is prohibited by law (Rule 3.4 (b)). It is professional misconduct for	A barrister must not rehearse, practise or coach a witness in relation to his evidence (Bar Standards rC9.4). A barrister must not call witnesses to give evidence or put affidavits or witness statements to the	Lawyers must not influence witnesses and experts. But such contact is allowed in arbitral proceedings when arbitration rules provide for it (Article 7). Article 25 (2) of the 2012 Swiss	An advocate and solicitor shall not interview or discuss with a witness, whom the advocate and solicitor has called, his evidence or the evidence of the other witness while such witness is under cross-	A solicitor must not advise or suggest to a witness that false or misleading evidence should be given nor condone another person doing so; or coach a witness by advising what answers the witness	

IBA Guidelines on Party Representation 2013	ABA Model Rules of Professional Conduct 2013	Bar Standards Board Handbook (England and Wales) 2015 and Solicitors Regulation Authority (SRA) Code of Conduct 2011	Rules of Professional Conduct of the Swiss Bar Association 2005	Singapore Legal Profession (Professional Conduct) Rules 2012	Australian Solicitor Conduct Rules 2012	Council of Bars and Law Societies of Europe (CCBE) Code of Conduct 2013
that an expert report reflects the expert's own analysis and opinion (Guideline 22). A party representative should not invite or encourage a witness to give false evidence (Guideline 23). A party representative may assist a witness in preparing for their testimony in direct and cross-examination, including through practice questions and answers. Such contacts should however not alter the genuineness of the witness or expert evidence, which should always reflect the witness's own account of relevant acts, events or circumstances, or the	a lawyer to engage in conduct involving dishonesty, fraud, deceit or misrepresentation (Rule 8.4 (c)).	court which he knows, or is *instructed*, are untrue or misleading (Bar Standards rC6.2). Unless permission of the representative for the opposing side or of the court is given, communication with any witness (including clients) about the case while the witness is giving evidence is prohibited (Bar Standards rC9.5). A solicitor shall not attempt to influence a witness, when taking a statement from that witness, with regard to the contents of their statement (SRA Indicative Behaviours 5.10). A solicitor must not be complicit in another	Arbitration Rules provides that it is not improper for a party or its counsel to interview witnesses, potential witnesses and experts.	examination (Rule 62 (1)). This shall not prevent the advocate and solicitor from communicating with his client for any purpose necessary to the proper management of the matter being handled by him (Rule 62 (2)). An advocate and solicitor may interview and take statements from any witness or prospective witness at any stage in the proceedings, whether or not that witness has been interviewed or called as a witness by another party to the proceedings except that if the	should give to questions which might be asked (Rule 24.1). A solicitor must not confer with any witness (including a party or client) called by the solicitor on any matter related to the proceedings while that witness remains under cross-examination (Rule 26.1). Exemptions are made when the cross-examiner has consented beforehand or the solicitor believes on reasonable grounds that special circumstances require such a conference (Rules 26.1.1 and 26.1.2).	

	expert's own analysis or opinion (Comments on Guidelines 18–25; Guideline 24).		person deceiving or misleading the court (SRA Outcome 5.2).	advocate and solicitor is aware that the witness has been called or issued a subpoena to appear in court by the other party to the proceedings, he shall inform the advocate and solicitor of the other party of his intention to interview or take statements from the witness (Rule 66).		A solicitor must not take any step to prevent or discourage a prospective witness or a witness from conferring with an opponent or being interviewed by or on behalf of any other person involved in the proceedings (Rule 23.1).	
Misconduct	The tribunal will consider claims of alleged misconduct and can take appropriate measures (Guidelines 26 and 27).	It is professional misconduct for a lawyer to violate or attempt to violate the Rules of Professional Conduct, knowingly assist or induce another to do so, or do so through the acts of another (Rule 8.4 (a)).	The Professional Conduct Committee will consider claims of alleged misconduct and will bring it before the disciplinary tribunal (Bar Standards Section A 3). A solicitor must report to the SRA promptly, serious misconduct by any person or firm authorised by the SRA (SRA Outcome 10.4).	There are no rules regarding misconduct in the Singapore Professional Conduct Rules.	Syndicates can consider claims of misconduct (Article 31).	A breach of these Rules is capable of constituting unsatisfactory professional conduct or professional misconduct, and may give rise to disciplinary action by the relevant regulatory authority, but cannot be enforced by a third party Rule 2.3).	There are no rules regarding misconduct in the CCBE Code of Conduct.

Interaction of IBA Rules with major institutional rules

IBA Guidelines on Party Representation 2013	LCIA 2014	ICC 2012	SCC 2010	SIAC 2013	ICDR 2014	WIPO 2014	HKIAC 2013
Candour and honesty							
A party representative should not make any knowingly false submission of fact to the arbitral tribunal (Guideline 9). A party representative should not submit witness or expert evidence that he or she knows to be false (Guideline 11).	A legal representative should not knowingly make any false statement to the arbitral tribunal or the LCIA court (Paragraph 3, Annex to LCIA Rules 2014).	There are no prescribed rules for counsel regarding candour and honesty in the ICC rules.	There are no prescribed rules for counsel regarding candour and honesty in the SCC rules.	There are no prescribed rules for counsel regarding candour and honesty in the SIAC rules.	There are no prescribed rules for counsel regarding candour and honesty in the ICDR rules.	There are no prescribed rules for counsel regarding candour and honesty in the WIPO rules.	There are no prescribed rules for counsel regarding candour and honesty in the ICDR rules.
Communication with tribunal							
Unless agreed otherwise by the parties, a party representative should not engage in any ex parte communications with an arbitrator	During the arbitration proceedings, a legal representative should not deliberately initiate or attempt to	All pleadings and other written communications submitted by any party, as well as all documents annexed thereto, shall be supplied in a number of	There are no prescribed rules for counsel regarding communication with the tribunal in the SCC rules.	All statements, documents or other information supplied to the tribunal and the registrar by one party shall simultaneously	No party or anyone acting on its behalf shall have any ex parte communication relating to the case with any arbitrator, or	No party or anyone acting on its behalf shall have any ex parte communication with any candidate for appointment as	No party or its representatives shall have any ex parte communication relating to the arbitration with any arbitrator, or with any

IBA Guidelines on Party Representation 2013	LCIA 2014	ICC 2012	SCC 2010	SIAC 2013	ICDR 2014	WIPO 2014	HKIAC 2013
concerning the arbitration (Guideline 7).	initiate with any member of the arbitral tribunal or with any member of the LCIA court making any determination or decision in regard to the arbitration (but not including the Registrar) any unilateral contact relating to the arbitration or the parties' dispute, which has not been disclosed in writing prior to or shortly after the time of such contact to all other parties, all members of the Arbitral Tribunal (Paragraph 6, Annex to LCIA Rules 2014).	copies sufficient to provide one copy for each party, plus one for each arbitrator, and one for the Secretariat (Article 3.1).		be communicated to the other party (Rule 16.6).	with any candidate for party-appointed arbitrator, except to advise the candidate of the general nature of the controversy and of the anticipated proceedings and to discuss the candidate's qualifications, availability, or impartiality and independence in relation to the parties, or to discuss the suitability of candidates for selection as a presiding arbitrator where the parties or party-appointed arbitrators are	arbitrator except to discuss the candidate's qualifications, availability or independence in relation to the parties (Article 16).	candidate to be designated as arbitrator by a party, except to advise the candidate of the general nature of the dispute, to discuss the candidate's qualifications, availability, impartiality or independence, or to discuss the suitability of candidates for the designation of a third arbitrator, where the parties or party-designated arbitrators are to designate that arbitrator. No party or its representatives shall have any ex parte communication

	Guidelines	LCIA	SCC	SIAC	WIPO	HKIAC
					to participate in that selection. No party or anyone acting on its behalf shall have any ex parte communication relating to the case with any candidate for presiding arbitrator (Article 13.6). Documents or information submitted to the tribunal by one party shall at the same time be transmitted by that party to all parties (Article 20.5).	relating to the arbitration with any candidate for the presiding arbitrator (Rule 11.5). All documents or information supplied to the arbitral tribunal by one party shall at the same time be communicated by that party to the other parties and HKIAC (Rule 13.3).

Information exchange and disclosure

	Guidelines	LCIA	SCC	SIAC	WIPO	HKIAC
	The party representative should inform the client of the need to preserve, so far as reasonably possible, relevant documents (Guideline 12).	There are no prescribed rules for counsel regarding information exchange and disclosure in the LCIA rules.	There are no prescribed rules for counsel regarding information exchange and disclosure in the SCC rules. The Rules provide for examples of case management techniques e.g. avoiding requests for document production when appropriate in order to control time and cost	There are no prescribed rules for counsel regarding information exchange and disclosure in the SIAC rules.	There are no prescribed rules for counsel regarding information exchange and disclosure in the WIPO rules. The tribunal and the parties should endeavour to avoid unnecessary delay and expense while at the same time avoiding	There are no prescribed rules for counsel regarding information exchange and disclosure in the HKIAC rules.

(cont.)

IBA Guidelines on Party Representation 2013	LCIA 2014	ICC 2012	SCC 2010	SIAC 2013	ICDR 2014	WIPO 2014	HKIAC 2013
A party representative should not make any request to produce, or any objection to a request to produce, for an improper purpose, such as to harass or cause unnecessary delay (Guideline 13). A party representative should not suppress or conceal, or advise a party to suppress or conceal, documents that have been requested by another party or that the party whom he or she represents has undertaken, or been ordered, to produce (Guideline 16).		(Appendix IV d) (ii) or in those cases where requests for document production are considered appropriate, limiting such requests to documents or categories of documents that are relevant and material to the outcome of the case (Appendix IV d) (iii)).			surprise, assuring equality of treatment, and safeguarding each party's opportunity to present its claims and defences fairly (Article 21.1). The parties shall exchange all documents upon which each intends to rely (Article 21.3).		

Witness/Experts interviews and preparation

A party representative should seek to ensure that a witness statement reflects the witness's own account of relevant facts, events and circumstances (Guideline 21). A party representative should seek to ensure that an expert report reflects the expert's own analysis and opinion (Guideline 22). A party representative should not invite or encourage a witness to give false evidence (Guideline 23). A party representative may assist a witness in	Subject to the mandatory provisions of any applicable law, it shall not be improper for any party or its legal representatives to interview any witness or potential witness for the purpose of presenting his testimony in written form or producing him as an oral witness (Article 20(5)). A legal representative should not knowingly procure or assist in the preparation of or rely upon any false evidence presented to the arbitral tribunal or the LCIA court (Paragraph 4,	There are no prescribed rules for counsel regarding witness/expert interviews and preparation in the ICC rules.	There are no prescribed rules for counsel regarding witness/expert interviews and preparation in the SCC rules.	It shall be permissible for any party or its representatives to interview any witness or potential witness (that may be presented by that party) prior to his appearance at any hearing (Rule 22.5).	There are no prescribed rules for counsel regarding witness/expert interviews and preparation in the ICDR rules.	To the extent that a witness is given access to evidence or other information obtained in the arbitration in order to prepare the witness's testimony, the party calling such witness shall be responsible for the maintenance by the witness of the same degree of confidentiality as that required of the party (Article 69 (b)).

There are no prescribed rules for counsel regarding witness/expert interviews and preparation in the HKIAC rules.

(cont.)

IBA Guidelines on Party Representation 2013	LCIA 2014	ICC 2012	SCC 2010	SIAC 2013	ICDR 2014	WIPO 2014	HKIAC 2013
preparing for their testimony in direct and cross-examination, including through practice questions and answers. Such contacts should however not alter the genuineness of the witness or expert evidence, which should always reflect the witness's own account of relevant acts, events or circumstances, or the expert's own analysis or opinion (Comments on Guidelines 18–25; Guideline 24).	Annex to LCIA Rules 2014).						

Misconduct

The tribunal will consider claims of alleged misconduct and can take appropriate measures (Guidelines 26 and 27).	The arbitral tribunal may decide whether a legal representative has violated these general guidelines and, if so, how to exercise its discretion to impose sanctions (Paragraph 7, Annex to LCIA Rules 2014).	A party which proceeds with the arbitration without raising its objection to a failure to comply with an provision of the Rules, or of any other rules applicable to the proceedings, any direction given by the arbitral tribunal, or any requirement under the arbitration agreement relating to the constitution of the arbitral tribunal or the conduct of the proceedings, shall be deemed to have waived its right to object (Article 39).	There are no prescribed rules for counsel regarding misconduct in the SCC rules.	1) A party who knows that any provision or requirement under these rules has not been complied with and proceeds with the arbitration without promptly stating its objection shall be deemed to have waived its right to object (Rule 37.1).	There are no prescribed rules for counsel regarding misconduct in the ICDR rules.

There are no prescribed rules for counsel regarding misconduct in the WIPO rules.	There are no prescribed rules for counsel regarding misconduct in the HKIAC rules.

Index